Vessel And Voice

Being A Powerful

And

Effective Christian

In A

Post-Christian Culture

Jennifer Stengel-Mohr

The primary Bible version referenced in this book is the New International Version. Scriptures from other versions are noted next to the scripture.

ISBN: 978-1-957294-05-6

R.D. Talley Books Publishing, LLC
P.O. Box 271029
Las Vegas, Nevada 89127
www.rdtalleybooks.com

Dedication

To God, my Abba who has created me with power, love and a sound mind.

To Jesus, my Savior who makes my burdens light and gives me salvation.

To the Holy Spirit, who has guided me my entire life whether I was aware of it or not. I give praise and gratitude beyond words.

I am grateful to all the prayer warriors, teachers of The Word, friends and family for their endless love and encouragement.

I am most grateful to my wonderful husband who is the rock of our family and the hands and feet of Jesus. And to my amazing son who has grown to be a fine ambassador for Christ. I am blessed by your discernment and insights.

"I will declare your name to my people;
in the assembly I will praise you."

-Psalm 22:22

Preface

"For if I preach the gospel, that gives me no ground for boasting. For necessity is laid upon me. Woe to me if I do not preach the gospel!"

1 Corinthians 9:16, ESV

In my previous book, *Peace on Purpose*, I explored various scriptures related to living with the peace that only Jesus could provide. That book was a tool for reflection in order to make observations and transformations in how to tackle the various circumstances of life. It served to work within an individual. *Vessel and Voice* is about moving forward once we have transformed ourselves so we can make an impact for the Kingdom.

The Kingdom is at hand and within us. We need to work with God to bring Heaven down to earth, materializing God's Will for ourselves and His people. We are His hands and feet. Often, we might wonder where God is, as we watch the world fall into more depravity and decline each day. Yet God is asking, *where are we?*

We can take guidance from the story of David found in 1 Samuel. David knew God and believed God could save him from Goliath, yet David still needed to be the one to throw the stone. David needed to take an active role while still having faith that God would work in the situation. We cannot sit along the sidelines in life and pray that God will do all the work.

We must develop what He has placed in us, so we can become effective Christians and carry out His call on us to bring the Gospel to all of the world.

For most of us, this will not look like traveling across the world to some remote mission field. It is going to look like our workplace, our church, our community and our family. The current challenge is that we are now in a post-Christian culture, where the majority of the world is not really open to hearing from God or about God. However, we must press-on and share the Gospel through our words and actions daily.

Since my last publication, I have completed a Doctorate in Ministry with a concentration in Apologetics. It is from this experience along with the guidance of the Holy Spirit that inspired the content of this book. The knowledge that I gained had such a tremendous impact on me that I knew I was not to keep it for myself, but to share it with others.

I pray that what is shared in this book ignites your passion for the Gospel, calls you to action, equips you to move forward and glorifies God!

Table of Contents

Introduction

We have to recognize that we are on a mission. We have been put on earth for a purpose. If you are reading this, you have been chosen by God to be His. There is a fallacy of belief that everyone is God's child. While everyone is His creation, not all are called to follow. This is a sobering realization about humanity. Some, no matter what experiences they have or what facts are presented to them, will not submit to the realization of God and even fewer will be chosen. As Jesus spoke in Matthew 7:13-14, "narrow is the way" and "few will enter".

Over time, I have come to be aware of just how narrow the gate is that Jesus spoke of. While God desires to have all His creation worship and love Him, He has created us with free will and He simply will not go against His character to force someone to choose Him. We can be led, but ultimately, we must choose. God in His mercy will give this opportunity until the end of time (Acts 2:21). God does, however, bestow special favor on those who have chosen Him. He then equips those people to withstand the evil forces of the world that has turned against Him.

God gives us supernatural abilities to make us the salt and light in the darkness of earth. So, if you have accepted Christ as your Savior, you are chosen, set-apart, and equipped to handle whatever comes into your life here on earth. You are also aware that this choice provides you with life eternal with the everlasting, Almighty God.

Comprehending all this is just one aspect of being chosen. We must also understand that with God's power and protection comes responsibility. Like David, we must do our part. That includes living a life of excellence that is devoted to praising and honoring God. We are commissioned to share Jesus with everyone we meet. And, we are to hold back the demonic forces that are at work daily throughout this earth. We do this as the Holy Spirit leads, by the power and authority of God. Sometimes this means doing nothing when we want to speak-out and other times it requires us to take a stand. Once we grasp this part of the choice we made, we begin to live a life that is powerful and effective for the Kingdom of God.

Make no mistake: it is clear in John 15:19. Because we are chosen by God, we will be hated by the world. I have personally experienced this many times. As someone who lives according to traditional Christian values, I have experienced first-hand what it is like to be set apart from this world during my many years of teaching in the public school system. Having had these experiences for over two decades it has given me extraordinary insights into how other people think and act, when they are "of the world".

This secular worldview includes a diversity of ideologies and insights. While they are all different, one thing that unites them is that they are so vastly distinct from the biblical worldview.

In my professional capacity, I am able to acknowledge and respect all of these viewpoints. Yet, I personally cannot partake in them or be part of their dissemination. To do so would compromise my moral obligation to my God, who has set me apart. Therefore, I must do all I can to stand firm and hold back the forces that are pressing against me in this environment. One thing is for certain: in such an instance, we cannot lose our compassion or integrity for how we deal with those who think differently than us. This is how we live out the example Christ gave us.

I've often found myself being a minority in the collective thought process within my work environment. At times, I have had to remain silent when there was an error in thinking, knowing full well that my voice would be seen as inciting discord. Yet in other instances, the injustice and absurdity was so great, that I had to speak up as to not be swallowed up into an abyss of harmful thinking. This is where we must strike a balance. We can only be balanced if we are grounded.

Sharing these accounts are not to complain or claim persecution, but to illustrate that these experiences have refined me, strengthened my faith and provided me with skills on how to navigate a post-Christian culture.

That is not to say that I have not been harassed for my biblical worldview. In some cases, persecution was spoken. Other times it was subtle, like a disapproving stare for wearing a cross necklace. I have taken it all in stride. Based on scripture as my foundation, I am going into these situations knowing that I irritate the demonic forces that are controlling the earthly realm. I can stand because the power that lives inside of me, through Jesus Christ is greater than the forces on the outside.

With the example above of wearing the cross necklace, why is it that this offends others? It certainly could not be attributed to a "religious" intolerance issue, when there was a large Buddha statue in the main office of my job glaring down on everyone. No one complained about that. There are no issues when the Muslim students seated outside my office are on their prayer rugs. That doesn't offend anyone. Yet, the cross on my physical person was somehow offensive to others. So, if "religious" tolerance is in fact being practiced in this environment, why was the cross so offensive? Simple, it represents THE Truth! Jesus is the way, the truth, the life. For those living in darkness, they do not want to be reminded of the light. It forces them to face the truth, something they do not want to embrace.

So, how did we get to this point? Not to turn this into a history lesson, but we must understand that historically, much of this country possessed Christian values.

This meant that we could live our life the way we were comfortable to and still blend-in. We are now in a time when this is no longer the case. Therefore, as followers of Christ, we have two choices: we can try to fit ourselves into society and go along with their ways or we can set ourselves apart and uphold the ways of scripture.

The former choice is the path of the least resistance. It is easy to just be apathetic and continue on. This is also the path of compromise and will cause us to erode away the values that we once held dearly, and it may even cost us our soul. On the other hand, the latter choice is a daily uphill battle. It will be met with hardship and hurt. If we set ourselves apart, we will surely be ridiculed, maybe outcasted or even persecuted in some form for that matter. Yet, this is the road God will meet us on. He will be there in the struggles if we are on the path to righteousness. Again, using Jesus as our example, while staring at the cross, He did not choose the easy way. He chose the righteous way.

Besides the work of the cross and our salvation through Christ, the most important part of God's story is that He loved us enough to create us with free will. So regardless of the worldly details, the fact of the matter is that it comes down to our choice. It is always for us to decide if we are for God or against Him. As all of the martyrs of history know too well, even if the law of the land is against God, we can still choose to be for Him, being fully aware that every choice has its consequences. The significance of understanding this is tremendous.

This totally wipes out any and all excuses to doing something against God's Will. We sin because we choose to. That is why we need Jesus. And since we have all sinned, that is why everyone needs to hear about the freedom and redemption that comes from choosing Jesus.

Having free will is tricky. Our choices are only authentic if it is an informed choice. That means we need to be operating with knowledge and facts that are truthful and trustworthy in making that choice. What many people are overlooking is that all of life is a battle over truth. The world has its truths and God has THE TRUTH. Satan cannot undo the work of the Gospel. That victory is complete! But he can deceive people by making counterfeits, manipulating it or lying about it. The world, which belongs to Satan, is selling counterfeit gospels.

As believers, we hold God's Word, the scriptures as absolute truth. It is the measure by which all of our decisions should be made, and this is where the conflict arises from. All other world viewpoints do not acknowledge, believe or know that God's Word exists. Therefore, at the heart of their decision-making there is already a major flaw. Currently, this is the dominant viewpoint in the world. So, we are daily contending with others who, at the core, think very differently than us.

With all that said, it would sound like we should pack-up our belongings, head for the hills and start our own community. But we are specifically told in scripture we are to not hide ourselves, but rather bring others to the light.

Jesus said in Matthew 5:15, "Neither do people light a lamp and put it under a bowl. Instead they put it on its stand, and it gives light to everyone in the house." If we evacuate our jobs, schools, communities and churches, it creates a void and more darkness will creep in. Jesus went into the communities and sat with the people who lived less that godly lives. He was showing us how we conduct the business of the Kingdom.

As discussed, we are now in a post-Christian culture. After centuries of literature, art and progress chiefly spear-headed by Christian thinkers, we are now faced with a dominant worldview that is increasingly secular. What is most disturbing is that it has come to light that many people who are calling themselves Christians, do so in name only. That is, at the core, their beliefs do not reflect what is widely accepted as Christian doctrine. According to a recent Barna study, one quarter of the self-described Christians actually had a view of God that was inconsistent with scripture. [1]

There is such a confusion and warped sense of what it means to be Christian. In some cases, being Christian simply means trying to live as a 'good' person without any real biblical basis for such assumptions.

---

[1] https://www.barna.com/research/most-american-christians-do-not-believe-that-satan-or-the-holy-spirit-exist/

Yet for others, being a Christian has become associated with evil, intolerant ideologies where believers are seen as hateful. This is a serious concern and there are two main reasons we are seeing this happen. In many ways we have been ineffective and powerless as the true body of Christ. First, we have become complacent through our prosperity and have compromised our morals in order to not make waves in society. It begins with allowing infringements against God's Word to be overlooked within our own homes and churches. This has snowballed, crashed and left a muddy puddle not resembling Christ's spotlessness or God's holiness. We have been living in ways that are not pleasing to God and have misrepresented God to the world. Not only is the world confused about who God is, but many "believers" are as well.

The second main reason for loss of Christian values is that, as the body of believers, we have consistently given up ground in all the major spheres of influence. Christians once held key roles of influence in areas such as education, politics and culture. These positions have slowly disappeared and have been replaced with extremely ungodly alternatives.

We need to gain ground! We must coalesce as a united body of believers and stand firm, refusing to give up any more ground or freedoms. If Jesus has set us free, then we should be free indeed. Surely, we cannot do this without God being in it and going before us.

While Jesus was on earth, He suffered every trial we could imagine. He was well aware what it was like to walk this life as a human. Yet, Jesus prayed to The Father on our behalf and said, "My prayer is not that you take them out of the world but that you protect them from the evil one" (John 17:15). With Jesus interceding for us while we are here on earth, we can have confidence that God has given and will continue to give us what we need to withstand the forces of this world and the plans of the enemy. Prayer will be one of our key tools in this battle.

So hopefully, you are with me in hunkering down, rolling up our sleeves and getting to the business of the Kingdom. The scriptures and insights in this book will start to pave the way for you to create your own plan of how to move forward. The title of this book was conveyed to me so clearly in the spirit. One day I was particularly stressed about the events going on in the world and I cried out to God, what can I do? I felt in my spirit God saying "I need you to be you. Be my vessel and voice."

A vessel needs to be empty in order to be filled-up. God wants us to empty ourselves so He can fill us with the Holy Spirit. Only once we are filled by Him can we pour into others. A vessel also protects whatever is inside. It is not about the vessel, but what it is carrying that matters. Not only are we a vessel for God's Spirit, but for His Word, which is truth. Finally, a vessel is strong yet not unbreakable. It needs to be treated well and handled with care as to not break it. We need to be preparing and protecting our vessels to be ready for battle.

As for voice, it can be loud or soft and still be effective. Our voice has the ability to calm people and motivate people. A bold voice speaks truth. Lastly, a steady voice can lead people out of darkness. We are to use our voice to bring people to Christ. The world is trying to silence our voice. That does not necessarily mean we should speak louder, rather we must learn to speak more effectively. We need a clearly refined voice guided by the Word of Scripture and the power of The Holy Spirit. We need to understand who we are, what we believe and how to effectively use that to win hearts for Jesus.

This book is structured in a way that will support your journey as you develop your vessel and strengthen your voice. The book is divided into three sections.

Section One- Will build understanding of what we believe about God and ourselves. We must sure-up our foundation, which is in Christ. We need to understand who God is and what His plan is. Chapter 1 focuses on the first essential step which is understanding God's Character. You will find keys in chapter 2 on discernment, which is knowing how to identify truth. We learn to define ourselves by daily reading of scripture. The remaining two chapters in section one address our conflict of being in the world but not of it. By knowing more about our identity in Christ we gain power to resist the counterfeits of the world.

Section Two- After building a foundation, this section addresses how to refine our voice as we share the Gospel in the location where God has placed us.

We will explore how to embrace the Holy Spirit who gives us power, how to effectively use our words to share Jesus with others and how to increase our boldness to share our testimony.

Section Three- Will give you tools for defending the faith and for putting on the Armor of God so you can fight this battle daily.

Throughout the book, each chapter begins with a pivotal verse as its foundation. I encourage you to read this verse and pray for God to bring you revelation about it. The end of each chapter also contains three segments to support your pursuit of that chapter's topic in more depth:

- **For your Heart-** includes the key points and scriptures from the chapter to meditate upon.
- **For your Spirit-** includes a prayer for focusing your spirit to commit and submit to God.
- **For your Mind-** includes additional resources to consult if you want to explore the topic further.

This journey is something God has chosen you and equipped you for. Don't let what you see in the world distract you from who God is and who He made you to be. Satan is aware of these things and works overtime to prevent them from becoming a reality. It is long overdue that we should be working overtime, too. It is my sincere hope that you become a representative of The Word, not of the World.

We are on this journey together and I am agreeing in prayer with all who read this that we will become mighty and effective for the Kingdom, in Jesus' name.

Section One

Defining Ourselves:

Developing A Foundation and Preparing Our Vessel

We can only know who we are by knowing who God is!

Knowing God and His Character

God said to Moses, "I AM WHO I AM"; and He said, "Thus you shall say to the sons of Israel, 'I AM has sent me to you.'"

Exodus 3:14 (NASB, 1995)

God is not a monolithic entity. He is vastly dimensional and, even within our highest intellectual human capabilities, we cannot fully comprehend all who God is. Understanding the nature of God is extremely complex and our human limitations only allow us to scratch the surface of understanding His magnificence. Even non-believers have preconceived notions of who God is or is not. What we need to be cautious of is that we do not try to fit God into our belief system and limit who He is, based on what we think we know.

All of scripture proclaims who God is! It would be impossible to narrow down one verse to define Him. However, when God spoke of Himself to Moses, He calls Himself "I Am". This is such a foundational understanding because He is the beginning and end of everything. This verse also shows us that God is in the present. He is not *I was* or *will be,* but the *I am* of the continuous present.

Our words are not even enough to fully explain the magnitude of God. God declares in Isaiah 55 verses 8-9, "For my thoughts are not your thoughts, neither are your ways my ways, declares the LORD.

[9] For as the heavens are higher than the earth, so are my ways higher than your ways and my thoughts than your thoughts." While we cannot completely define Him, we can understand His character by His words and actions all throughout scripture.

God is Holy. He is set-apart. That is why it would be impossible to bridge the gap between ourselves and Him without Jesus. Due to our sinful nature, we would have no business being in the presence of our Holy God. Yet, God was willing to come to earth to save us so we could have a relationship with Him. No other belief system or religion serves a god who humbled himself to save his people. There is only one, the true God, the great *I Am*. How can God have such mercy for a people who have continually disobeyed and even denied Him? It is out of love.

Love compelled God to have a redemptive plan for His people since the beginning. We are able to perceive love because He first loved us (1 John 4:19). If we understand this part of His nature, it makes it clearer who we are and what we are called to do. God did not create us and then walk away, rather He walks with us. He is a very real presence in our daily life. If we seek Him, He will be found.

Love is the first element in a good relationship. Because of the love God has for us, we should feel that love in return, therefore having a desire to serve Him, rather than feeling obligated to do so. If we really believe in this and desire this type of reciprocal relationship with God then we must extend God's love to others.

God is in need of nothing from us, so the way we serve Him is by serving others. Jesus says in John 21:16, "Simon, son of John, do you love me?" He answered, "Yes, Lord, you know that I love you." Jesus said, "Take care of my sheep."

Beyond love, God's nature is so immense and all consuming that not enough books could be written to contain all that He is. However, in this chapter we will focus on some of the key elements of His nature to better understand why God must be central to everything we do if we truly desire to be effective and powerful in this life.

God does not view the world as we do. He does not divide it as secular vs. religious. All aspects of life are under the jurisdiction of His Will. Colossians 3:23 states, "Whatever you do, work at it with all your heart, as working for the Lord, not for human masters". This scripture is clear that although we are called to various roles and assignments here on earth, we are to always have a Kingdom perspective. This perspective keeps us in alignment with God. When we are in such an alignment, it gives us access to knowing Him better and benefiting from all the blessings that come from Him.

God's Will is revealed in Exodus when God gives Moses the laws that would establish His Kingdom with the Israelites. Not only does God deliver the Ten Commandments, which are moral laws, but He gives Moses the civil laws for how to govern and judge and also the ceremonial laws for worship. Each of these laws reveal to us God's character and a demonstrate how holy He is.

But what is most important is that they are given to us out of love. God intends the best for us and these laws and guidelines establish healthy and holy parameters to live as God's people. It is interesting to note that within the Ten Commandments, the first four are about our relationship to God. Commandments 5-10 are concerning our relationship with others. The God of all creation reveals that our relationship with Him is of primary importance. That says a lot about who God is.

God is infinite, uncreated and His Kingdom is eternal. This sets up the understanding that God is far bigger and grander than anything else in existence. As humans, we cannot even fathom God's perspective based in eternity. This is where faith bridges the gap in our understanding. Based on God's Word, we must believe in His promises in our spirit because our mind is too limited to fully comprehend.

So, when we face a challenge in life that might seem immense and overwhelming to us, for God who sees eternity, it is merely a blip on a screen. That does not diminish the significance or legitimacy of that event because ALL things work together for the good of those who love God (Romans 8:28), but rather it can give us a perspective of how this one event stands in relation to eternity. Then we might understand how to better respond to these circumstances with a Kingdom mindset. God cares about all the details, both big and small. He sees the struggles we face and He is in it with us.

The vastness of God is manifested in the fact that He is omnipotent, omnipresent and omniscient. Nothing happens on earth or in heaven without God knowing about it or allowing it. Since we are in a fallen world, bad things happen. These things are a result of the consequences from the choices we collectively make. When choices are made against God's Will, we see that they result in non-favorable outcomes. While God might not choose the difficult things to happen in our life, He does allow them so we can learn to depend on Him. Knowing He is always with us should give us the confidence we need to address the difficulties before us.

God is everywhere at all times. He is omnipresent. This is possible because God is spiritual not material. In Psalm 139:7-10, David says, "Where can I go from your Spirit? Where can I flee from your presence? [8] If I go up to the heavens, you are there; if I make my bed in the depths, you are there. [9] If I rise on the wings of the dawn, if I settle on the far side of the sea, [10] even there your hand will guide me."

God is not bound by the laws of physics. Coupled with the fact of being eternal, at any given moment, past, present or future, God is there. This should give us great hope that no matter the circumstances, God is with us in that place and time.

God is all knowing, He is omniscient. Psalm 147:5 states, "Great is our Lord and mighty in power; his understanding has no limit."

Surely with this being true, it should be easy to trust Him because He knows how it all works out. Again, this is where our faith is applied. We say we trust Him, but we still want to entertain the thoughts in our mind of how we think things should be. Letting go of ourselves and letting God step in is the best thing we can do in our life. Abandonment of our need to know and control every detail in our life is so liberating. Completely turning everything over to God and trusting Him solely will make us powerful and effective believers. For if we do, then we are unburdened with all our baggage and God can do amazing things within us and through us.

God is all powerful. He is omnipotent. God says in Jeremiah 32:27, "I am the LORD, the God of all mankind. Is anything too hard for me?" We often like to tell God how we think things should go. Yet, it is His Will that will prevail. We can try to escape this truth and work within our own capacities, but this often ends in disappointment. When we leave God out of our process, we deny His power and simultaneously weaken ourselves. When we align ourselves within God's Will, we get access to the flow of His power through the Holy Spirit.

It seems futile to have access to God's immense power and yet not incline ourselves to tap into it. Submitting ourselves to God's power and authority doesn't diminish us, it empowers us to walk with Him in power.

Because of God's sovereignty, all power, wisdom and authority are His. Colossians 1:16-17 tells us, "For in him all things were created: things in heaven and on earth, visible and invisible, whether thrones or powers or rulers or authorities; all things have been created through him and for him. [17] He is before all things, and in him all things hold together." Putting God at His rightful place in our life is where our strength, power and efficacy come from. We must never act alone, but under the full direction of God according to His Will.

This brings to mind an important discussion that believers often banter about: Can God do miracles? Absolutely! Does he still do them? Yes! Under God's authority, can people perform miracles? Also, yes. But God does not dispense miracles like an ATM. We must be careful how we use the authority given to us by God. While we can have supernatural powers bestowed upon us, we need to be careful to not act as though we are God.

Another important characteristic of God is that He is unchangeable. He is the same yesterday, today and for eternity. So, we know His Word will stand forever and His promises can be trusted. For us to entertain any other 'truths' is futile.

The world and its people offer many promises they cannot uphold or have the right to promise in the first place. Our only firm foundation is in the Word of God.

Acts 17:24-31 (ESV) gives us a beautiful description of God, His intentions and our purpose; "The God who made the world and everything in it, being Lord of heaven and earth, does not live in temples made by man, [25] nor is he served by human hands, as though he needed anything, since he himself gives to all mankind life and breath and everything. [26] And he made from one man every nation of mankind to live on all the face of the earth, having determined allotted periods and the boundaries of their dwelling place, [27] that they should seek God, and perhaps feel their way toward him and find him. Yet he is actually not far from each one of us, [28] for 'In him we live and move and have our being'; as even some of your own poets have said 'For we are indeed his offspring.' [29] Being then God's offspring, we ought not to think that the divine being is like gold or silver or stone, an image formed by the art and imagination of man. [30] The times of ignorance God overlooked, but now he commands all people everywhere to repent, [31] because he has fixed a day on which he will judge the world in righteousness by a man whom he has appointed; and of this he has given assurance to all by raising him from the dead."

Seeking God is as vital to our walk on this earth, as it is for our eternity. We must seek Him while He can be found (Isaiah 55:6-7). The challenge lies in the fact that the more we find, the more we want to know and our knowledge of God will not be complete until we are on the other side of eternity. But, the desire to keep seeking and knowing should be the fuel that moves us each day.

There are many mysteries within the faith, but God reveals to those who desire an earnest understanding of whatever we wrestle with. I've personally experienced this in my health journey so many times. I could not understand why I was chronically ill. Why was I allowed to be sick? Didn't God want me to be well so I could do more for him? I had so many questions and for many years, I tried to rationalize these notions in my own head. One day, I felt so strongly in the spirit, God saying, "Why aren't you asking me?"

I have conversations and prayer with God all the time, but it did not occur to me to ask Him the questions that were difficult and weighing heavily on me. I was looking for answers from everywhere except from Him. He is a good Father and does not want us to be distressed. If we truly believe in the relational God, we must open up the lines of communication and wait for Him to respond. Communication is a key component to seeking him with all our heart, mind and spirit. In response to my seeking, I found that in the times of my greatest physical distress from my illness, I was the closest to God and He was the closest to me. Obviously, I do not desire to be ill, but I do not resent it either. It has been one of the main reasons why my faith has become so strong.

God may not heal my physical body, but He has made me well. I have seen God move again and again on my behalf in all aspects of my life, but specifically in my health issues. It has strengthened my relationship with Him in amazing ways.

Another great mystery of the faith is the Trinity. The Trinity further reveals the nature of God in three persons. God is one being in three persons: Father, Son and Holy Spirit. All three are present since the beginning of existence and will remain for eternity. The pattern of a trinity can be found in many natural realities, such as nature, family and science. Although there are three essences of God, they act in oneness and cannot exist without the other. While this concept does take some knowledge to understand, scripture provides wonderful insights into each and how they work together.

God the Father is the creator of all things. He is the first person of the Trinity we see in the first verse of Genesis. There is no other entity in existence higher than Him. It is from God that we receive everything. James 1:17 tells us, "Every good and perfect gift is from above, coming down from the Father of the heavenly lights, who does not change like shifting shadows." He is Abba, daddy from whom love and discipline flows. He is the mastermind behind the plan to save His people and bring about the gloriousness of His Kingdom.

Jesus the Son is the Redeemer. This is the person whom God has sent to take on flesh and walk this earth to bring God's love down from heaven. Jesus is the only door that leads us to God and the bridge that narrows the distance between us and Him. Jesus is the one who is continually interceding for us on our behalf. It is only through the Son that we may know God The Father.

The Holy Spirit is God's spirit that is poured out into us. He is the comforter, helper and advocate that Jesus asked His Father to send us so we would not walk alone. It is the Holy Spirit that makes known to us the thoughts of God. He is the one who tells us how to pray when we do not know how. We are told in 1 John 4, that the Spirit living inside us is greater than that which is in the world. The Holy Spirit is the source of our strength.

Although all persons of the Trinity are independent, they function together and need to be part of our life together. We must embrace all three persons for who they are to us and pray towards all three in unity.

Knowing all of this about God is overwhelming, so how are we to respond? Hebrews 12:28 tells us, "Therefore, since we are receiving a kingdom that cannot be shaken, let us be thankful, and so worship God acceptably with reverence and awe." Daily worshiping God in reverence and awe places Him in His rightful place in our lives and puts us in a position of strength.

Believing in God is not the same as being a worshiper of God. Satan himself believes in God. Worshiping God must be in fullness, in love and without exemption. This is essential to who we are as individuals. In Luke 10:27 (ESV), Jesus was asked about what is most important as believers. So he answered and said, "You shall love the LORD your God with all your heart, with all your soul, with all your strength, and with all your mind,' and 'your neighbor as yourself.'" So, if we love God, we must love others. That is how we know we are His.

For Your Heart

- *God is the source of everything. He is loving, sovereign and eternal.*
- *Without Jesus we cannot get close to God.*
- *God is for us, with us and ahead of us.*

For Your Spirit

Father God, I praise you endlessly for your goodness and I am in awe of your magnitude. I want to get to know you more deeply. Thank you for sending Jesus to bridge the gap in our relationship, so that I can come to you boldly with this request. Lead me in the knowledge of you and correct me in any way where I have erred. Although your ways are so far beyond what I can imagine, I pray that I will never lose my desire to keep pursuing you. Thank you for your patience with me on this journey. -Amen

For Your Mind

The Nature and Character of God- W.A. Pratney. (1988) Bethany House Publishers. MN

Knowing His Voice

"Whoever is of God hears the words of God. The reason why you do not hear them is that you are not of God."

John 8:47 (ESV)

Since we were being formed in the womb, our sense of hearing has been developing. Before birth, a baby can recognize its mother's heartbeat and even her voice. At birth, a newborn can immediately recognize and respond to sounds with a complete and functioning sense of hearing. Our eyes, on the other hand take time to open and adjust to the environment around us. It is so amazing how God has created us. It is built into our DNA to listen first! We are reminded several times in scripture not to base our reaction on what we see, but on what God's Word says. Our eyes can deceive us, so we should be led by His voice.

God's voice will always speak two things: love and truth. He is speaking to us through His Word and Spirit all the time. The trouble is, are we listening? Most of the time God whispers. He is the still small voice that directs us in the way to go. However, God can speak in a loud, thunderous voice, but if you have heard this then take heed. He is definitely trying to get your attention and it is usually a warning. Only when we have ignored His whispers will He get out the bull horn. Delayed obedience is disobedience. So, when God speaks to us, we should respond quickly.

We can only recognize God's voice if we know God's Word. This requires a deep and continual reading and study of scripture. We need to have internalized scripture so that it is within the fiber of our being and is part of who we are. Therefore, when a situation presents itself, we do not need to delay. The Spirit will lead us in what to do if we are listening.

There are three voices in our head: ours, Satan's and God's. We need to be able to identify which voice is controlling the airtime. Most of the time, we entertain our own thoughts or voice. Occasionally, Satan will creep in to plant doubt, fear or lies in order to throw us off track. One way to know which voice is vying for control is to look at the motivation behind the voice. If it is self-serving, then it is our voice. If it is aligned to scripture, then it is God's voice. If it is contrary to scripture, that it is the enemy. Again, knowing this only comes from having a solid foundation in God's Word.

Satan is the master of deception. Nothing he says is truth or can be trusted. He is the source of the original sin and fall of man. Therefore, entertaining his voice, even momentarily, can have dire consequences. Satan is also the king of counterfeits. He has no creation powers so he can only mimic and manipulate all that God has done and created for his own purpose.

This is why Satan is so crafty. On the surface his voice can sound appealing or even correct. Yet, upon closer examination of his proposition, we see the many flaws of how it is not in our best interest and it is leading us away from what God has for us. The way you can spot a counterfeit is by studying the original. We need to get so well-versed in scripture that we can spot an errancy a mile away.

This is why we need to be at the top of our game when it comes to discernment. Charles Spurgeon, a well-respected evangelist said, "Discernment is not being able to tell the difference between right and wrong but being able to tell right from almost right." Our discernment needs to be as fine as a grain of salt. Imagine if a recipe called for ¼ cup of salt, and due to a momentary distraction, you grab the sugar instead. They both look the same, yet they are very different and serve different purposes. This mix-up would have significant consequences on the outcome of the recipe. We must not be distracted by the things of this world, so much so that we can no longer hear God's voice. Even more so we cannot confuse the voice of this world for the voice of God. Surely, that will have dire consequences.

Because we may be so busy and distracted, we can often miss what God is revealing to us. What I find most helpful is to write down what I hear God 'speak' to me. I keep a journal while reading scripture and praying so that I can record and refer back to the interactions that I have had with God's voice.

This allows me to hold it up to scripture, test it and meditate on what He has said to me. It then becomes a source of information to help me make good decisions or to help support someone else. Much of what is in this book comes from these 'conversations' with God.

The daily war we wage is in our own minds as we battle the voice of the world. Society is operating on a different set of "truths". Sometimes the world (or the enemy) can sound convincing and almost morally correct, yet if you hold it to the plumb line of God's Word, it is totally out of alignment. Therefore, we can be sure that it is not truth and it is not God's voice.

Jesus tells us in John 10:27-28, "My sheep hear my voice, and I know them, and they follow me. 28 And I give unto them eternal life; and they shall never perish, neither shall any man pluck them out of my hand." Once we have accepted Jesus, we are His. Therefore, He can call to us and we will know it is Him. Choosing to follow Jesus as our example and continually listening for His leading through the Holy Spirit will increase our discernment for truth.

It is said that the top three voices in our life are the ones that are most influencing our thoughts. So, who are those voices for you? Is there a specific preacher, social media influencer, professor, parent, friend that you "follow" or hang on their every word? Hopefully, at least one of those top voices is Scripture, the voice of God.

We must ask ourselves, what is our source of information and truth? Traditionally, the most influential sources for truth for most people have been education, media and/or church. These were considered pillars of truth in society. The assumption was that your teachers and professors would not knowingly give you misinformation. The media could be trusted for accurate representation of facts, details and events. And the church was sacred, so they would not mislead or deceive you. However, we have consistently witnessed the steady erosion of these pillars at an alarmingly fast rate. The only truth that has not changed over time is The Truth of God's Word. The promises of scripture are still true today. God does not change and neither does His Word.

Testing what we hear is important. Truth will always bear good fruit. So, we only need to observe what fruit is being produced by the knowledge and information being imparted. If the information leads to death, destruction or chaos then it is safe to say it was not truth. Truth will lead to life, abundance and peace. The traditional pillars of truth in society have fallen so far from God's Truth which has led people and nations to destruction.

First, let's examine the pillar of education. The current curriculum within a majority of public schools leaves a lot to be desired. Academic integrity aside, let's consider the social, moral and emotional components of many of the current curricula.

In kindergarten classrooms across the country, you can find five-year olds being taught sex education. Exploring sexual feelings and discussion on why it is okay to question sexual identity is not developmentally appropriate for this age group. There is not one single justification for why this should be entertained or why more people are not outraged by this.

There are first graders being read stories of families with same-sex parents. As in the previous example, this is entirely inappropriate for this age group. In a classroom, teachers are seen as the authority, therefore what they say lends validity to what is shared. These ideas become normalized by the impact of repeat exposure. Teachers share it, peers talk about it and the media exploits it.

By the age of ten, students are being informed in schools that they have a right to pick their gender, without any knowledge or intervention by the parents. What a child says to a social worker, teacher or medical professional is private and does not need to be communicated to the parents because it would violate the rights of the student. These students are being spurred-on to be thinking of such things by voices that are not from God and are not serving the students' best interest. Students are in school an average of seven hours a day. In many cases, this is more time than they have contact with their parents and families. These voices will speak loudly in a child's life solely due to sheer quantity of exposure.

Fourteen-year olds are being convinced that abortion is empowering. Young girls are led to believe the right to choose to kill an unborn baby is the ultimate sense of control. A belief that a woman's status is determined by how much authority she has is what drives the focus of this issue to be about the choice-making rather than the choice, in this case life and death. This partially stems from the self-centered view we have in society. Even if this is not the prevailing belief in the home, a girl cannot escape the overwhelming pressure to conform and embrace this powerful identity while in this environment.

As if this information is not shocking enough, all this "instruction" is carried out without parental consent and, in many cases, without parent knowledge. The reason for this outrageous indoctrination is simple: the voice of influence in education is not aligned with God's Word. That voice is not just a little out of alignment, it is counter to it. This agenda, which has not been hidden, is to turn the minds of the children toward darkness. We are painfully aware that if they capture the mind of the child, it is difficult to undo that impression. Proverbs 22:6 (KJV) tells us, "Train up a child in the way he should go, and when he is old he will not depart from it." So, the question is, whose voice is doing the training?

These previous examples are just some found within the K-12 educational environment, which serves children under 18 years old. Not one of these ideas is in alignment with God's Word and is therefore, not truth.

Yet from an early impressionable age, the children are being molded and shaped by these ideas being fed to them through the system. This is not just a one-off experience, but rather a regular diet of such ideas, not only being taught by those in charge, but also being reinforced by their peers. Under this type of structure, often a child cannot withstand the pressures to question, rebuke or abstain from this indoctrination. This fact coupled with the other two pillars of truth spreading the same lies is a recipe for disaster. Even when a child comes from a Christian home environment, it is extremely difficult for them to operate outside the thought of the system.

So, let's examine the fruit of such systemic instruction and thinking. Since Christian values and prayer have been taken out of the public schools, around the early 1960's, we have seen a steady increase in bullying, school-aged suicide, drug and alcohol use, school shootings and a decrease in graduation rates. This is not what God intends for the children He loves. We are witnessing the consequences of bad decision-making and choices that were made in the absence of truth. Those with power to make choices are not acting with the children's or society's best interests in mind, nor are they adhering to God's voice in these decisions.

Indoctrination of ungodly thought is a regular diet within the K-12 system and it is creating children who are malnourished academically, morally and socially.

In addition, the voice of parents is being drowned-out over the noise of the subversive agenda. What parents have failed to realize is that there is no such thing as a public education. The reality is that it is a government education and those in power are the voice that speaks to the children in the manner they choose and for the purposes they see fit.

With that being said, we must be careful not to villainize the teachers, who in many cases are swept up in this craziness as well. While there are some who actively pursue pushing this agenda, what happens is largely out of the teachers' hands. The teacher unions and the political special interest groups are the ones who are making the real decisions that have tremendous impact on the children.

There are two ways to address this challenge. First, we must take back influence over the school system. Parents should be involved in having their voices heard. This requires representation of the Christian values to be part of the decision-making process. Being on school boards and in school meetings is essential. There needs to be a presence and pressure in order to make things change. If you cannot be in one of these positions, consider adding the people who are onto your prayer list. Pray for them to listen for God's voice and have courage to stand against things that are not of Him. Being active in local politics can also have impact over this situation as well.

If our voice is represented locally, then that will trickle into matters at a local level, like school boards. Remember, you do not need to be a parent to be a concerned citizen.

Secondly, if you do have school-aged children, consider home education. There is a tremendous movement towards home schooling. What was once seen as underground and extreme has now become very mainstream. My husband and I home schooled our son from third grade through high school. It is not for everyone and it is not easy, but the benefit is unquantifiable. It provided an opportunity for our family to make every choice directed by God's voice, it made us closer as a family and gave our son such a well-rounded educational experience. The experience facilitated freedom and encouraged self-reliance in terms of knowledge-building. At 21, our son is now able to stand firm against schemes of the enemy because he can examine things from a multitude of perspectives. As a result, he can converse with the world as equally as well with the believers without compromising his worldview.

Home schooling has been given some negative stereotypes in the past, but that image is shifting as people realize that having control over your child's learning environment when they are impressionable is not only a God-given right, but a prudent decision for the life of the child and the future of the country.

Home schooling should not be seen as sheltering children from the big bad world, rather it is about being mindful of how and when the child is getting information that will be age appropriate and within a context that can be discussed in light of the family's worldview. It is about preparing children to receive knowledge and experiences that are appropriate for a time in which they are ready for them. Choosing to home school and keeping your child from the system weakens the overall power and influence the system can have. It sends a clear message and exercises your voice as a parent to have control over the welfare of your child. In addition, it creates a remnant of children who will think differently from the rest of the world. They are the future and the stronghold for the Christian voice.

Looking at higher education brings a whole other set of concerns. Non-biblical ideological thought is prevalent on many campuses and has infiltrated every academic area. Honest debate and discussion are stifled and replaced with compliance or cancelation. One is perceived foolish to even suggest that God exists. A recent study showed that far-left professors outnumbered conservatives by 8:1 in full rank positions and 49:1 in junior rank titles.[2] The implication of this is that for thousands of students, the voice they are regularly filled with is in direct opposition to the Word of God.

---

[2] Ellis, John, "The Breakdown of Higher Education". (2021) Encounter Books, New York, p.26

Here again, the agenda is also coming from top-down powers, yet the professors serve as political activists to the captive audience of their students. Professors who support the non-biblical worldview see it as their civic duty to taint any content they teach with the underpinnings of social theory. It is not about facts, truth or knowledge, it is about control. Getting students to think like they do is the goal. There are no areas within education at this level that are not impacted by this sense of obligation. This is occurring within the areas of science, math, and technology, where you would expect a more purist approach to the content itself. However, lessons are rarely about the knowledge within that subject matter, but how to use that knowledge for social justice and/or political gain.

Clearly there is much work to be done within education to redirect the course it is currently on. Awareness is key. First, bringing our concerns for these issues to God in prayer is essential. Obviously, this is not because God is unaware, but rather it shows God that we have become aware and we are on His side. He will then in turn give us the tools and strength we need to stand against the evil and make His voice heard once again in these spaces. Awareness also helps to unite like-minded individuals to stand firm against the agenda that is infiltrating the school system from Pre-K through college. A united front is a symbol of strength and with God behind it, it will have impact.

On a practical level, it will be critical to get involved where we can so God's voice is seated at the decision-making table. Looking for opportunities to correct and educate others in these concerns will be necessary. Surely, things won't change overnight but we could derail the agenda and potentially scale back its impact a little at a time.

On to the next pillar of information, the media, which is at an entirely different level. One need only to reflect on the recent events of the global pandemic to realize media may not be an accurate depiction of reality or truth. For two years we observed how every day the story changed based on who was telling it. The level of manipulation in media during this time was unprecedented. What makes this a heavier lift than the area of education is that now we are dealing with corporations and an obscene amount of money. This is big business, where pedestrian influence is almost non-existent.

With media's far-reaching tentacles, the shear influence they have over every facet of our lives is immense and they know it. Full advantage has been taken to carefully construct truths that will change the way people think and respond to daily world events. Whoever controls the media controls the voice of the entire world.

Given the dynamics of media, it is much more difficult to make room for God's voice to be the prevailing influence when other aspects of society have been so effective in removing His very existence.

God has been taken out of schools, the justice system, sports games and all public places. The narrative that the God of the Bible is a fairytale or an ancient myth, and not relevant for modern times, is a prevailing thought. Since the very thought or existence of God has been widely dismissed, it becomes easy to sell a new narrative that makes people the god of the day.

We need to hold the media accountable for their impertinent attitude for information and for how they represent it. There is only one way that is possible in this case. Our voice is our money. We must stop patronizing the media outlets and corporations that support the media's bad choice-making. Once there is a genuine commitment from believers to step away from these ungodly platforms, impact will be felt financially and inroads can then be made for change. This goes in tandem with additionally supporting the sources and corporations that do not try to silence the voice of God and His people.

The last pillar of perceived truth, the church, is a delicate matter. It was once believed that church was a safe place where God's truth was celebrated and aspired to. However, it is well known that it has also been a source of hurt and mistrust for many people. The church has done its own share of misleading both in biblical and secular matters. One way has been with their silence. Many churches have refused to take a stand to support biblical truth in daily issues. This has left their congregation vulnerable to enemy attack.

J.C. Ryle, states in his book, *Holiness,* "Myriads of professing Christians nowadays seem utterly unable to distinguish things that differ. Like people afflicted with color-blindness, they are incapable of discerning what is true and what is false, what is sound and what is unsound. If a preacher of religion is only clever and eloquent and earnest, they appear to think he is all right, however strange and heterogenous his sermons may be. They are destitute of spiritual sense, apparently, and cannot detect error."

It is clear that a voice other than God's has infiltrated the walls of the church. From pulpits, some pastors have even adopted non-biblical viewpoints and are using their platform to lead people astray in world affairs. And there are some "churches" that are teaching another gospel entirely. They have distorted, or all together, changed the true meaning of the scriptures. We must recognize if God's voice is even absent within a multitude of churches, we really have a problem.

Let's examine what fruit comes when the church moves away from truth. There has been a steady decline in church attendance for decades. A recent Barna study states that Christianity has undergone dramatic change over the last few decades.[3] It is now believed that only 1 in 4 Americans is a practicing Christian. These numbers should not be a total shock when we look at society.

---

[3] https://www.barna.com/research/changing-state-of-the-church/

If we only make up 25% of the population, it is difficult to command 100% of the truth. This is why it is critical that when believers are showing up to church, the voice of God is the only thing speaking to the people. Every church must teach the uncompromised Word of God without fear or pressure from the rest of society. If it is not, then they are no better than the rest of the world and they are bringing destruction to the congregation.

Because of careless preachers and confusing voices within the church, countless numbers of believers have left the faith or are in a process of deconstruction. Deconstruction is when a believer takes a step back to evaluate what they believe. Not that this is inherently bad, but most often this leads to a path of atheism. The believer not only backslides but turns from the faith completely. Clearly this not only impacts the individual believer, but everyone who interacts with this backslidden individual as well.

Again, as with schools, this is not to say that there are not churches that are in fact bold in standing for the uncompromised Word of God. There are many, along with so many wonderful churches that are harvesting souls daily for the Kingdom. But at its core, the church has been shaken and many people are on the surface skeptical, if not completely turned-off, to the idea of church being a pillar of truth. The voice of God, through the church has lost its effectiveness. It is for us to be sure to carry His voice into every interaction we have daily, speaking as a representative of the Kingdom and biblical worldview.

Therefore, if our traditional sources of truth have been compromised, where can we turn? We must go back to what God intended anyway. It comes down to His Word, our heart and the Holy Spirit. Martin Luther, during the reformation, never intended to break away from the Catholic Church. He was focused on making the church aware that they had moved far away from what scripture says. Luther's mantra was "solo scriptura", only scripture. Once we start to derive the truth from any other place than its original source, we run the risk of being led astray.

How do we know God's Word is the absolute truth? Because it has been tested. It is consistent, it reflects reality and it has stood the test of time. God's voice is the same yesterday, today and tomorrow. If we are operating under any other "truth" then we are being misled and are not able to have the power we should because our foundation is weak.

The real question is, do **we** believe this is absolute truth? This is obviously not a concern for the unbeliever. It is for us! Do we believe in all the promises of God found in scripture? If yes, then we must depend on it daily. We are to listen to God's voice and do what it says. James 1:22 reminds us, "Do not merely listen to the word, and so deceive yourselves. Do what it says." The measure of our belief comes in how we live it out.

For Your Heart

- *God always speaks truth and love.*
- *God can whisper or shout.*
- *He communicates to us through His Word and Holy Spirit.*

For Your Spirit

Father God, thank you for creating me in such a way that I can continue to have a relationship with you and hear all that you have to say to me. I ask that you hone my ability to hear you. Give me discernment to know Your truth. Please let me walk in Your will and Your strength. In Jesus' name I pray. -Amen

For Your Mind

10 Things Satan Doesn't Want you to Know- John Van Diest, Colorado: Multnomah Publishers (1998)

The Breakdown of Higher Education- John Ellis, New York: Encounter Books (2021)

How Do You Kill 11 Million People? Why The Truth Matters More Than You Think- Andy Andrews, Tennessee: Thomas Nelson Publishers (2011)

Knowing Ourselves- Culture vs. Character

"But to all who did receive him, who believed in his name, he gave the right to become children of God, who were born, not of blood nor of the will of the flesh nor of the will of man, but of God."

John 1:12-13 (ESV)

We are in a tug of war as humans. The world is so loud and bold in assigning labels and identity to each and every person. Labels are a way of knowing who you are and where you belong. Your label can get you into a group or exclude you from a group. Do not be distracted by these labels. As followers of Christ, we must understand our identity is in Christ. If the world gives us our identity, then they can take it away just as easily. If our identity is tied to something of this world, such as our job title, social status or relationships, if one of those things change or no longer exist, then how would we define ourselves?

In Christ, we do not change our identity because things shift within our environment or in our emotions. We are who we are because He is who He is! This identity is solid and powerful. It gives us the ability to serve our role within this world in an effective manner. Regardless of our title, serving God is our Job!

While reflecting on the events in my life, I noticed one thing they all had in common: me! Whether the outcomes were good or bad, at some level I was responsible for how things turned out.

It could have been my direct actions or just my attitude toward the situation that made all the difference. I have to recognize the consequences of my choices and learn from them.

The post-Christian culture feeds off the blame game. Pointing fingers at others for poor decisions made by oneself, all the while claiming to be the victim in the circumstances. God did not assign us the role of victim. He has made us victorious through Christ. Therefore, we need to act in such a manner to claim the victory, whether it be in the natural result or in our spirit, knowing we will overcome.

The power God gives us through our identity in Christ is no surprise to the enemy (John 1:12-13). This is why the enemy, through the channels of society, is on the prowl robbing people's identities through manipulation, confusion, and deceit. As a result, we have seen such a tremendous increase of young people questioning their identity. The world is celebrating their confusion and cheering them on, right off the side of a cliff. Satan knows that if you question your identity given to you by God, then you are weakened. An identity crisis is something that can break a person, and Satan is counting on it.

We can easily fall into this identity crisis when our focus is on ourselves. In the post-Christian culture, we are worshippers of self. It has become a prevalent mindset in our society. You only need to view a moment of social media to realize this fact. The invention of a "selfie" says it all. This represents a shallow and empty view of self.

It is superficial and focused on how the world perceives us. We have become a society of people-pleasers and this does not please God (Ephesians 6:7).

Jesus walked in humility. His thoughts were always for others and not Himself. Again, a sign of His abundant love. If we can harness a fraction of His humility, it would serve us well as a society. C.S Lewis said, "Humility is not thinking less of yourself, it's thinking of yourself less." What most people don't realize is that self-obsession is self-destructive. This is building our life on a shaky foundation. Surely, after a few storms, the house will come crashing to the ground. But building our life on Jesus is a sure foundation. This begins with us understanding who we are in Him.

Since we are obsessed with ourselves, our words and actions follow in suit. A popular catchphrase that accompanies this mindset is the reminder that "you are enough". This is particularly preached to and targeted toward young women. Its goal is to empower women to embrace an identity that defies the true beauty God created women to be. It preaches a false sense of self-sufficiency, pride and even entitlement. This is another example of false thinking that is being celebrated by the masses as people are being crushed by the deception of this mantra.

The truth is, we are not enough. We could never be enough and that is why we so desperately needed a savior in Christ.

If we are trying to get through this life on our own strength and merits, we might as well give up now. Jesus must be our foundation if we are to succeed.

It follows logically that in an obsession with self, moral relativism would fit the narrative. Moral relativism is the plague that is sweeping through the post-Christian culture. It is a belief that there is no absolute truth or set of morals that exist outside of ourselves. It is a belief that humans create their own judgements based on their personal will and desires. Therefore, the individual gets to define the rules in which they operate within the world.

It should be obvious that this belief is incapable of producing a society in which there is harmony, health or safety for all of its members. If everyone does what they feel is "right", then it becomes, in essence, a free for all. All things, including identity and behaviors, are at the whim of how people feel in the moment. The truly sad part of this mindset is that those who are caught up in it are not aware of how oppressed they are in their belief. They are unaware of how destructive this mindset is for themselves and for society.

We must be the stop-gap for this type of thinking until Jesus' return. This is where our identity in Christ needs to radiate the brightest. As believers, we must stand firm and live a life that tells a different story. We need to adhere to the biblical morals and truths as if our life depends on it, because it does.

Refusing to get swept-up in the moral mire is our obligation. Saying yes to Jesus means saying no to the world. We must not bend for fear of ostracization.

We are reminded in 2 Timothy 1:7 (NKJV), "For God has not given us a spirit of fear, but of power and of love and of a sound mind." After mediating on this verse for some time, I saw a vision of *The Wizard of Oz*. This was one of my favorite stories growing up. Even until this day, it holds value and enjoyment for me. We are all familiar with the moral of that story as Dorothy often repeats it, "there is no place like home." What we have to remember is that this earth is not our home. Being seated with Christ in heaven is where we belong. So, while we are here, we are just on a journey until we reach that destination. This is the first realization of our identity in Christ and it should give us perspective on so many of life's issues. If we remove ourselves from the temporal, we begin to see in the eternal. This is when we take on a Kingdom mindset, which transports us to a higher reality of who we are in Christ.

Going back to the story, you probably also remember the other main characters were on a quest for three things. The Lion was looking for courage, The Tin Man for a heart and The Scarecrow for brains. Not having these qualities was a severe detriment to each characters' ability to succeed in their journey. Fortunate for us, as told to us in 2 Timothy, God has already equipped us with all of these things. He has given us power, love and a sound-mind.

Therefore, we do not need to fear how we make it through this life on our way towards home. We can confront the witches, wizards and storms with confidence because of who God created us to be and the tools He has given us for the journey.

Like in the story, things were not what they seemed once the curtain was pulled back. Jesus did not pull back the curtain, He tore it down and ripped it in half. This not only reflected His power, authority and identity, but signaled the change that His life, death and resurrection would usher in. Because of what Jesus did on the cross, we do not need to look to the world to bestow anything on us. God has already seen to giving us all we need. Our assignment is to recognize and properly apply what we have been blessed with. This realization sets us up to handle the challenges of life's journey from a much different perspective.

We must understand that culture is not constant. It ebbs and flows with the changing times and tides of this world. However, we know that God and His Word does not change. He is the same yesterday, today and forever. Therefore, we should have confidence in our position in Christ regardless of life's storms. Approaching daily life from a Kingdom perspective puts God at the center of everything and reduces our potential to capsize in the rough seas. Our thinking needs to extend beyond the now. A Kingdom perspective means that we can live in the now while we prepare for eternity. This shift in thinking drastically changes how to address everything in our life.

No matter what our beliefs are, something will lord over our life and take a prominent position in it. This could be our job, our relationships, money, status, self, you name it. Reflect on who or what that is for you. Jesus is the only true Lord and when we submit to Him, everything else falls into place under His authority. If something else is the lord of our life, then we become bound to it. When Jesus is our Lord, we have freedom. Jesus is The Way, The Truth and The Life. Any other belief will lead us astray.

It is the truth that sets people free. In John 8:31-32 (ESV), we are told, "So Jesus said to the Jews who had believed him, "If you abide in my word, you are truly my disciples, 32 and you will know the truth, and the truth will set you free." Unfortunately, it has been my experience that the majority of society is not striving to live by truth, but by what makes them feel good. Doing what feels good is temporal. Our emotions are fickle and fleeting. They cannot truly give us freedom. Rather our emotions can keep us strapped into the roller coaster of life, often making us wish we could stop the ride.

Operating based on what God's Word says rather than what is seen in this world will help us to rise above the circumstances before us. It does not mean we will not go through difficult times, because Jesus tells us we will (John 16:33). But we know that God is in the troubles with us and he will not let us fail.

This kind of confidence and faith goes back to what we believe about God and our relationship with Him. In order to experience this total freedom, we must be totally committed to God.

Commitment means love. We are told in Mark 12:30, "Love the Lord your God with all your heart and with all your soul and with all your mind and with all your strength." It is because we love God that we will choose Him over everything else the world has to offer. This requires our whole self to be in the process. Total commitment is not just saying 'yes' in our minds, but recognizing that every breath is because of Him and for Him. There should be no half-measures.

First, Jesus says we must love God with our whole heart. That requires God to be our first love. We can measure if this is true by looking at how we spend our time. Who or what is our time dedicated to? Ourselves? Others? A passion or pursuit? Seeking God early and often puts us in His presence and in the fullness of His love. Centering our hearts on God gives us a heart like His; one that is filled with compassion, grace and mercy. Having a heart that loves God means we recognize that He is the piece that makes us whole.

When we love God fully, it pours out of our hearts and into our minds. Many have tried seeking God through intellectual enlightenment alone. Yet, it is simply impossible to find Him purely through this intellectual pursuit because it is absent of relationship and love.

One may acquire wisdom along this journey which utilizes logic and reasoning to justify His existence, but they will not come to know Him or themselves.

Leo Tolstoy is a wonderful example of this. Tolstoy was a Russian Nobel Prize author who is best known for writing *"War and Peace"*. His insights on God are razor sharp and laser focused, yet he only committed to Christ in his mind. His studying and seeking only lead him far enough to recognize that Jesus was an intelligent and valuable teacher. Tolstoy believed Jesus lived as a real person. He agreed with His teachings yet did not accept Him as his savior (as far as we know). Therefore, after all the mental gymnastics, philosophical debates and deep intellectual searching, Tolstoy's salvation would still hang in the balance. It seems to me a rather vain pursuit to go so far in the journey of seeking God, but to miss out on the reward of accepting Jesus as a savior. I do pray that he received Christ in his final moments.

Jesus also revealed that total commitment is neither just a spiritual encounter while seeking God. We cannot just connect with Him on a spiritual plane. We must also have a knowledge and reverence for His Word. We must desire to dig deep into scripture and read it for ourselves, so we can know who He is and how we are to respond. This desire results in the ability to meditate on His Word day and night.

Jesus also points out that we need to love God with all our strength. That means our efforts need to reflect that He is our priority.

Can we honestly say that we have a love for God that is so deep that it will endure until our last breath? This is the kind of love Jesus speaks of. Once we have that, then we really understand who God has made us to be.

Understanding this complete commitment to God makes us keenly aware of the distinction between being a nominal Christian or being a follower of Christ. Recently, I have begun to move away from quickly giving myself the title of Christian. This label has become very murky and misunderstood. When asked about my faith, I say I am a follower of Christ. Besides, this is more accurate in the way I think and go about my daily life. It is a reminder to myself and a proclamation to others of who I live for.

In the same respect, we are probably very aware of our views towards others who are non-believers. But have we really contemplated what non-believers think about us? When a non-believer thinks about Christians, what is their view? One word that comes to mind is hypocritical. They may see us preach righteousness, holiness and devotion to God, yet in many ways we behave much like the rest of the world who does not recognize Him. Why would someone want to be part of a "religion" like that?

Regardless the label, our role is to be an ambassador for Christ (2 Corinthians 5:20). In this position, we must present ourselves as trustworthy and be able to live a life that reflects what we tell others we believe about God.

Philippians 1:27-28 tell us, "Whatever happens, conduct yourselves in a manner worthy of the gospel of

Christ. Then, whether I come and see you or only hear about you in my absence, I will know that you stand firm in the one Spirit, striving together as one for the faith of the gospel [28] without being frightened in any way by those who oppose you. This is a sign to them that they will be destroyed, but that you will be saved—and that by God." So, the question is, if we were to be put on trial for being a follower of Jesus, is there enough evidence to convict us?

Since we are a vessel, we will ultimately be filled with something. If it is not God's Word and His Spirit, then it will be something of the world. James 1:22 states, "Do not merely listen to the word, and so deceive yourselves. Do what it says." We cannot claim to be followers of Christ and then live completely contrary to what we say we believe, because that is hypocrisy. Our flesh will go with the path of least resistance, which is to be a follower of the world. We are only able to live alternatively when we know the truth of God's Word and allow the Holy Spirit to guide us in that truth.

Jesus says in Matthew 22:29, "You are in error because you do not know the Scriptures or the power of God." He was speaking to the Sadducees and correcting them because they were debating over Jewish Law from the Old Testament.

It is important to note that while the Sadducees were religious leaders, they missed the mark on two key points: they did not really know the truth revealed in God's Word and they underestimated the power of God. Jesus is speaking of this same power that is now in us through the Holy Spirit.

Often, we fall short when we are entertaining things of this world. When we try to look at the world from our human perspective, the flesh gives in. One defense we have is the Holy Spirit. He is our guide to navigate the snares of the world.

God has blessed us with our five senses so we can interpret and appreciate His beautiful creation. However, Satan is aware that these are our primary source of contact with the physical world and he has been on a quest to hijack them from the moment we were born. We must be so mindful of everything we allow into our field of perception. It only takes a small thread to unravel a sweater. If one area in our life is not in alignment with God's Word, it will have a ripple effect on everything else in our life.

There is nowhere that the post-Christian culture is more evident than in entertainment. While there is nothing inherently bad about technology, movies, music or any other genre of entertainment, the problem lies within the content of that entertainment. We have seen this area of society become increasingly anti-God and anti-Christian.

There is immense pressure to go along with the world on so many fronts. It is only the Holy Spirit and His conviction that will keep us on the narrow path.

If the things we allow into our lives (and our children's lives) do not align to what we know is good, true and pure according to God's Word, then we have no business dabbling with it (Philippians 4:8). Trying to justify hanging on to something of the world that is not in alignment with God is the evidence that we are not fully committed yet to Him. Because we have the Holy Spirit in us, we should have a disdain for these sorts of things. Immediately, our spirit should be grieved by what we are witnessing, which should make us turn from it.

A stumbling block to this is that we have learned to live with the "It's only" mindset. While it seems trivial, this is a very dangerous mindset. We rationalize that it's only a horror movie, it's only profane lyrics, its only sexually explicit, etc. Convincing ourselves that we can hold onto this world and hold on to God evenly is completely not possible. Jesus tells us that we cannot serve two masters. He says in Matthew 6:24, "Either you will hate the one and love the other, or you will be devoted to the one and despise the other. You cannot serve both God and money."

Although we might in some way like or enjoy this particular entertainment, partaking in it is a struggle of will. Do I do as I desire, or what God would want for me?

There is no difference between these choices and the choice Eve made in the Garden of Eden. God said 'no' and Eve said, 'it is only...a fruit.' We have to understand that everyday there is a series of these choices and each one is either leading us to God or away from Him.

In the book of Judges, when God calls Gideon to fight the evil of the Midianites, He first tells Gideon to go home and destroy the temple his father built to Baal. Even though Gideon was faithful to God, God would not use him to deliver the people until Gideon cleaned up the evil affairs within his own home and family. We cannot point fingers at the evil that is going on around us and complain while we are not willing to fix the evil that is happening within our own families, churches and communities. We must start with our own hearts and homes, then we transform outwardly.

What is helpful in harnessing the will to resist these worldly temptations is to consider the intentions behind them. They are not really designed to make you happy or to entertain you, they are to pull you ever so slightly away from meditating on the things of God. If it is not of God, then it is of Satan. A look at the people behind these industries tells you quickly that they are not promoting God's agenda. The enemy is behind each of these areas of culture and pushing the line further and further much more quickly than we have ever seen before.

We can also combat these worldly pressures by knowing our intentions when faced with them, deciding in advance that we will stay committed and stand firmly against anything that is not of God. This comes by knowing our faith is in God, not this world, knowing our hope is in Jesus, not any person, and knowing that life is not about this moment, but eternity. Each time we choose God instead of this world, we celebrate a small victory, each time becoming more and more of who God has designed us to be.

Who we are is not just about ourselves or what we get out of our life, but it is also what we give. We are called to be stewards of all the blessings, talents and gifts we have been entrusted with. We are conduits of God's power when we are using these blessings for His Kingdom and His people.

You may have heard the phrase, 'Mind the Gap'. This originated in London within the transportation system. It is a catchy phrase used to bring awareness to train riders about the open space between the platform and the train as it pulls into the station. It has since been used in a number of other circumstances, particularly in business. Entrepreneurs "mind the gaps" in product and service delivery in order to identify and create a unique business opportunity because nothing else exists like it in that space. I have learned to incorporate this idea into my daily approach to ministry.

The underlying premise is to look for the need. What is tugging at your heart? It is a good chance that this tug is a nudge from the Holy Spirit guiding you to where there is a need. We were not created to serve ourselves, but to serve others. Jesus is our example for this! Surely, if the Son of God came to earth as a servant, we should have the same expectation if we are His followers. Titus 3:14 teaches us, "Our people must learn to devote themselves to doing what is good, in order to provide for urgent needs and not live unproductive lives."

We are instructed in scripture to be the ones who care for widows and orphans. James 1:27 states, "Religion that God our Father accepts as pure and faultless is this: to look after orphans and widows in their distress and to keep oneself from being polluted by the world." One very dangerous shift we have seen take place over time is a change in the fact that individuals, communities and churches are no longer the primary source for meeting the needs of society. Because the church has not been diligent in fulfilling this obligation given in scripture, it has created a gap.

Other groups and particularly the government, which have very different worldviews, have now stepped in to fill these needs. We expect government-run social programs to take care of all of the ills of society. This is dangerous because it can create a power and control relationship for those who are distributing these resources.

It is also possible for the recipients to be bound to the system that is providing the resources to fill these needs. Rather than experiencing God's love by their needs being met, they experience loyalty to the hands that provided it. We must reclaim being the hands and feet of Jesus in a tangible way. We are created to be who we are because someone else is in need of exactly that.

Coming back to examining intentions, we should genuinely want to serve in any way we can because it is our opportunity to make God known to others. Philippians 2:3-4 states, "Do nothing out of selfish ambition or vain conceit. Rather, in humility value others above yourselves, [4] not looking to your own interests but each of you to the interests of the others." We are powerful and effective Christians when we do for others, not ourselves.

Being obedient to God and living according to how He has called us gives us strength even when we are faced with weakness. Life throws us many curveballs that try to weaken us and make us less effective. If we are aligned to God, He can strengthen us in every aspect of our life. Whether it be in our spirit, our relationships or our finances, God can move supernaturally even when the circumstances look very different. What is amazing about this type of strength is that it is not only impacting us, but others around us. People get to witness God through us.

When I consider how this has worked in my life, I envision it as an umbrella. Because I am under the umbrella of God's protection and provision, the world cannot destroy me. Therefore, I maintain my strength in the battle, and then in turn, I am able to help others. God is the god of multiplication. He can and will double our efforts.

We see this evidenced in scripture many times. It is evident in the feeding of 5,000. With two fish and five loaves of bread, thousands were fed by the hand of God (Matthew 14). Another example is with Paul and Silas when they are imprisoned (Acts 16). Their praises and faith in God not only set themselves free, but also broke the chains of all the other captives as well. We have the ability to bring others along for the ride in our journey. When we are aligned to God, we win big and others benefit.

Unfortunately, in contrast, this is also true if we are working counter to the will of God. When we do so, we create negative consequences in our life, which in turn can bring others down with us as well. This puts us in alignment with the enemy rather than God and we know that Satan, who steals, kills and destroys, is a master at division. So, when we align with him, we lose big.

The challenge is that sometimes it seems like the world's way is more enticing. In our sinful nature, we fall prey to the schemes of Satan that throw us off balance. We must remember that while we may lose a battle from time to time, we are guaranteed to win the war because Jesus has already claimed victory over that. It is important for us to not face the world as defeated, but as victorious.

So, between our identity in Christ and our identity in this world, there is simply no comparison. This world cannot offer us anywhere close to what we have through Jesus. Knowing this puts us in a position of power and authority right here and right now.

Choosing Jesus helps us let go of the empty promises of this world and embrace Him completely. Jesus made it clear that we are not in this alone because He interceded for us and still does. He says in John 17:14-20 (ESV), "I have given them your word, and the world has hated them because they are not of the world, just as I am not of the world. 15 I do not ask that you take them out of the world, but that you keep them from the evil one. 16 They are not of the world, just as I am not of the world. 17 Sanctify them in the truth; your word is truth. 18 As you sent me into the world, so I have sent them into the world. 19 And for their sake I consecrate myself, that they also may be sanctified in truth.20 "I do not ask for these only, but also for those who will believe in me through their message".

When we take on our identity in Christ there is nothing this world can dish out that can destroy us. Divine power, strength and wisdom go before us. We are under God's protection, covered by Jesus' blood and fortified by the Holy Spirit. Satan knows this. Do you?

For Your Heart

- *When we accept Christ, we become God's children who are loved and set apart for a purpose.*
- *We are ambassadors for Christ and therefore should conduct ourselves in a manner that represents Him well.*
- *In Christ, we are protected and empowered to encounter the circumstances around us.*

For Your Spirit

Thank you God for loving me and giving me redemption and salvation through Jesus. I pray that I glorify you in all that I do. I ask that I become aware of your presence as I fight the daily battles of life. I ask for your strength and wisdom in all life's circumstances. May I praise you all the days of my life. In Jesus' name I pray. -Amen

For Your Mind

The Dark Agenda- The War to Destroy Christian America- David Horowitz. (2018) Humanix Books. FL

The Plot to Change America- How Identity Politics is Dividing the Land of the Free- Mike Gonzalez. (2020) Encounter Books. NY

The Law of Love and The Law of Violence- Leo Tolstoy. (1948) Rudolph Field. NY

Knowing Our Purpose: Being Steadfast, Sagacious and Set-Apart

"Let your eyes look straight ahead; fix your gaze directly before you.
26 Give careful thought to the paths for your feet and be steadfast in all your ways.
27 Do not turn to the right or the left; keep your foot from evil."

Proverbs 4:25-27

I am aware that the title of this chapter is a mouth full, but perhaps it causes one to ponder a bit longer on the content of this chapter. This chapter is pivotal in the development of the power and effectiveness we desire. This is where the rubber meets the road. It is in the daily interactions and decisions where we will be tested. We must be simultaneously working towards being steadfast, sagacious and set apart in order to be powerful and effective for The Kingdom. Proverbs 4:25-27 addresses all three of these traits within these verses.

Proverbs 4 tells us to be steadfast in all of our ways. Being **steadfast** is to be devoted, faithful and dedicated to the work that is set before us. This is a call to be committed to the work of The Kingdom and diligently represent Jesus in all we do.

These verses also tell us to give careful thought to the paths of our feet, thus being **sagacious**. We must be wise, discerning and prudent in all of our decisions.

We are surely living in a time when we should test all things and weigh them against the Word of God. We must not look to the left or the right but stay focused on Him.

Additionally Proverbs 4:25-27 states, to keep our feet from evil. Since the world is evil, we must do our best to set ourselves apart from anything that can cause us to stumble. Being *set apart* does not mean we are recluse from society, but rather our thoughts, actions and words are to be distinguishable from the rest of the world. We should not get caught up with what the world says is right or how it operates, but rather be the example of what it means to be a follower or Christ.

We can more fully understand these traits in action when we look at the life of Jesus. Jesus possessed all of these traits. We will use His example to explore how worldly issues play out in light of these traits as our foundation. Jesus himself told us to seek first the Kingdom of God and its righteousness (Matthew 6:33). When Jesus walked as a man, he was singularly focused. His purpose was clear and He did not stray from it. Jesus was steadfast in bringing glory to God and fulfilling God's will. He did not do anything for Himself, but only according to the will of His Father. No matter what distraction or deception came His way, Jesus was unshaken and unmoved in His focus.

Jesus was so keenly aware of the eternal implications of the work that He was here to accomplish. It could be said, well of course Jesus was able to accomplish this, He was the Son of God.

While that is true, He stilled lived as flesh and because of him being fully man, He also had free will. Jesus could have chosen a different path. Jesus, prayed for His outcome to be different, but in the end, He chose God's will over His own. In John 10:17-18 Jesus says, "The reason my Father loves me is that I lay down my life—only to take it up again. ¹⁸ No one takes it from me, but I lay it down of my own accord. I have authority to lay it down and authority to take it up again. This command I received from my Father." The magnitude of this verse is tremendous. Realize that the entire fate of humanity was in the hands of one single person with one single choice. In that moment, Jesus chose us over Himself. Thank you, Jesus, for your sacrifice on behalf of all your people. This is why Jesus needs to be everything to us. He needs to be our singular focus because we were His.

In part, Jesus was able to be so steadfast because He was motivated by the most powerful force in the universe: love. Love is the currency of heaven. He loved The Father and He loves us. We see many verses in scripture that speak of Jesus' compassion for others. He did miracles and healed people out of His compassion. Therefore, as His followers, we too should be motivated by love. That is, that all of our actions are done with the right heart. Having this perspective will gives us a clearer focus for our purpose on earth, therefore making us more effective for the Kingdom.

A direct command from Jesus was to love God and then love one another. Here again is a representation of balance. What good would it be to claim to love God, yet show no care, concern or mercy for His people? We serve God by loving others. On the other hand, being a good or kind person to others is a nice idea, yet if we do not love God, nothing we do on this earth really matters. So, our concept of love must go vertical to God and lateral to others. When you put that together you get a cross and that is what it is all about. Jesus must be the center of everything!

Jesus demonstrated balance in His approach to every situation. He spoke and acted in truth and grace. His grace came from the love and compassion we just spoke of. His grace allowed Him to interact in such a way that although He had ultimate authority, He did not walk in pride or deal in a heavy-handed way. Each of Jesus' interactions and messages, while having authority, were conducted with grace and compassion.

God's Word is truth! Jesus is The Word made flesh, so He is the embodiment of truth and wisdom. As humans, we have a belief that "knowledge is power", but in actuality it is truth that has power. It is only when we walk in truth that we can possess power. Knowledge is only the information. It is when we use wisdom, the application of the knowledge, that we have an impact. Since God's Word is that truth, it should be the source of our wisdom. James 3:17 (NKJV) tells us, "But the wisdom that is from above is first pure, then peaceable, gentle, willing to yield, full of mercy and good fruits, without partiality and without hypocrisy."

Jesus demonstrated a wisdom that was beyond anything people had ever heard before and that is because He did not do anything on His own. Jesus never acted without the wisdom and guidance of His Father. Whatever else the world claims as truth is counterfeit and counterproductive. We have clear evidence of this fact as we look into the world. Counter to the Word in James 3:17, we observe corruption, war, division, conflict and hypocrisy that run rampant in the world. This is because it is not using God's wisdom as the basis for decision-making. It is only when we consult God's Word that we can know how to rightfully discern and decide how to respond to everyday circumstances.

Being sagacious is not just about the knowing, but about the doing. While having wisdom and truth, we cannot carry ourselves in a self-righteous manner.

We must strive to interact with kindness and compassion, especially with those who are non-believers. We might be their only encounter with Jesus, ever. In this lies the balance Jesus spoke of in John 17:16, of having to be in the world but not of it. Jesus did not move within the wisdom of the world, He moved in the wisdom of God. Therefore, He was set-apart.

Jesus was unlike anyone else who walked the planet and this irritated many people, especially those in power. Some just found Him strange, while others saw Him as a threat, which is why He was killed. Being set apart does not mean being isolated. While Jesus never sinned, he was often seen in the presence of those who did. Again, this is an example for us on how to be amongst people who think and live very differently from us without becoming them.

James 4:4 reminds us that friendship with the world's ways brings enmity with God. We must be distinguishable and set-apart from how the rest of the world thinks and behaves. Using the previously addressed principles of steadfastness and sagacity helps ground us in our faith and gives us the courage to stand apart from the world.

There is an immense amount of pressure from society to 'fit-in', but Jesus certainly did not demonstrate that at all. He came to show the world a different way. We are told in Romans 12:2 (NKJV),

"And do not be conformed to this world, but be transformed by the renewing of your mind, that you may prove what *is* that good and acceptable and perfect will of God." This scripture is often quoted, but what does it really mean?

Renewing our mind means to reshape it according to God's perspective, not the world's. The verb renew is in the present progressive tense, indicating that this is an ongoing process. Renewing is something that is required daily if we are to be set-apart from this world. This occurs through daily reading of scripture, communication with God through prayer and fellowship with other believers. The moment we take our eyes off Jesus, we slip into the ways of the world and it can quickly consume us.

A renewed mind is demonstrated in how we speak, think, act and respond to every interaction we encounter. Jesus has commissioned us to take over now to be the example for living a different way on this earth. Showing others that there is an alternative to acting and thinking like the world sets us apart. Because we can have this different perspective, it puts us into a position to also recognize and point out things that are not in alignment with God's Word. While we are not called to judge, we are called to rebuke and correct error.

This perspective also helps us to avoid entertaining extremes that can move us away from God's intentions. In Christianity today, we see extremes in a number of areas. These imbalances cause divisions within the church. We are warned in scripture about such divisions.

Paul speaks of such issues in 1 Corinthians 1:10; "I appeal to you, brothers and sisters, in the name of our Lord Jesus Christ, that all of you agree with one another in what you say and that there be no divisions among you, but that you be perfectly united in mind and thought." Here again, it is a collective renewing of the mind so that our eyes are fixed on Jesus, the Living Word. When we stray from that, we lose our foundation and that makes us imbalanced.

In scripture, we are called to be like-minded as believers. Romans 15:5 (NKJV) points out, "Now may the God of patience and comfort grant you to be like-minded toward one another, according to Christ Jesus". If our doctrine identifies us as a follower of Christ, then we should be united. We should not argue over distinction in details but stay focused on Jesus. These distinctions have been another source of division within the church. Denominations that split hairs over how believers worship distracts us from what really matters. When we are distracted, we are less effective and vulnerable to attack.

However, this does not mean that as believers we should be accepting of everything that comes into the church. We should be able to engage in critical discussion and debate about legitimate concerns facing the church, both from the inside and out. Questioning practices and traditions in accordance to how they align with what scripture says is critical to the survival of the church. Taking guidance from Jesus, these matters must be addressed with truth and grace.

One thing that is for sure: we should not blindly be in a church that runs counter to anything in scripture. Many churches have become like Hollywood. They preach the message that will fill the seats, which means what you are receiving might not be biblical. We cannot let our guard down when it comes to discernment, especially in a church setting. It is made clear in Jude that the enemy is already within the walls of the camp and is looking for someone to devour (Jude 4). Satan is using the church and the people within it to manipulate God's Word. We are warned many times in scripture to be on the lookout for false prophets and teachers. The entire book of Jude is dedicated to this topic of identifying and dealing with false teachers and doctrines.

We must know scripture well and practice discernment when looking at how an individual or church behaves. More importantly, when this type of imbalance occurs within a church, it tends to misrepresent God to others, as well. We must keep our eye on what is happening within the church more so than what is happening outside the church. We know there will be problems and corruption in the world. That will never change. We need discernment to weed out dangerous views within the church that threaten its existence and its effectiveness.

One sign we need to be watchful of is when churches go to extremes that take the focus off Jesus completely and place it onto the religion, the tradition or something else.

We want to be alert and sober-minded to avoid being disillusioned by experience or tradition, both of which can fall victim to manipulation by Satan and man. We are told in scripture to test everything (1 John 4:1).

Just because, a particular act of worship has been practiced in a traditional church for centuries, does not make it pleasing to God. On the other hand, modern experiences and encounters into spiritual realms can also be very dangerous. We cannot trust that our senses are always accurate, since they can be easily manipulated.

We will look at two extreme examples as points of illustration. First let's examine extreme fundamentalists views. While it is essential to have a strict adherence to scripture and its accuracy, this view tends to focus on who gets it "more-right", wanting to call out who is more righteous among believers, and the answer, as scripture states, is none of us. This view of God may be obstructed by legality and rigidity. This view works mostly from a logical and rational stance and does not have power. It can be so fundamental that it denies the power of the Spirit. This doesn't allow room for God to work within us and through us. The Holy Spirit is necessary to fulfill God's will on earth. He allows us to move supernaturally which we cannot do in flesh alone, even if our minds believe with all their might about how God works. If we are dormant in our use of the Holy Spirit, we simply cannot be set apart from this world.

For further illustration, we can examine extreme charismatic views and we find the exact opposite. This view is so "filled" with the Holy Spirt, that the focus is on the experience and what they are doing, rather than on Jesus and what He has done. These believers tend to desire the experience as proof of the power.

However, we have all the proof we need of the power in the Word. This adventure seeking type of faith is dangerous because it is centered around our feelings and senses, which can be misleading and manipulated. This is by no means a denial that the Holy Spirit does work through people. He surely does even today, but when He does it is for the purpose of doing God's work, not simply for our own gain.

Once we go to an extreme, we may not even be identifiable as Christians anymore. Christ can become so distant from the focus of the ends that it is not about Him at all. This is a very perilous situation to be in. One of the scariest sections of scripture for any believer should be Matthew 7:21-23 (NKJV), when Jesus says, "Not everyone who says to Me, 'Lord, Lord,' shall enter the kingdom of heaven, but he who does the will of My Father in heaven. [22] Many will say to Me in that day, 'Lord, Lord, have we not prophesied in Your name, cast out demons in Your name, and done many wonders in Your name?' [23] And then I will declare to them, 'I never knew you; depart from Me, you who practice lawlessness!'". We do not want to find ourselves saying we believe one thing and practicing another.

In between these extremes is the balance that keeps us focused on Christ with the knowledge of God's Word and the filling of the Holy Spirit which allows us to apply it. Being balanced also helps us to easily spot where this is an imbalance. This can provide us with an opportunity to bring those who are walking in this imbalance or darkness to the light.

Part of this imbalance is a result of the human struggle in keeping balance between fear and hope. While we are living in the physical world we are easily tossed by the storms of the day. Our body is programmed for protection and survival, which includes a certain element of fear for our own caution. However, fear taken to an extreme is paralyzing. It robs us of hope and joy. So, knowing what we know about the enemy who comes to steal, kill and destroy, we know that this unhealthy fear is one of his schemes. Satan is using fear to keep us suppressed from the power and effectiveness we possess by being set apart by God.

What has happened in recent history, primarily as a result of the pandemic, is that the world has been working overtime to pump fear into the hearts and minds of all people, leaving them in a state of learned helplessness. People have resigned to that fact that things are what they are, and little can be done to change that. The world has us fearing so many things, except what is to be feared most: God! We will address this fact a little later in the chapter.

Since we as humans are flawed, we carry these flaws into the church. We must remember that even though church leaders are ordained by God, they are still human and can fall to the same vices and wrongful thinking as anyone else. We need to be even more careful if we are in such positions. Scripture gives a warning to leaders and teachers that they will be judged more harshly because wrong thought not only harms ourselves, but those who follow us (James 3:1). Are we as a church body counteracting these fear tactics in a biblical manner?

Similar to Proverbs 4:25-27, we are also told in Joshua 1:7-9 to remain focused and not be distracted left or right, but to be strong and very courageous. Joshua says, "Be careful to obey all the law my servant Moses gave you; do not turn from it to the right or to the left, that you may be successful wherever you go. [8] Keep this Book of the Law always on your lips; meditate on it day and night, so that you may be careful to do everything written in it. Then you will be prosperous and successful. [9] Have I not commanded you? Be strong and courageous. Do not be afraid; do not be discouraged, for the LORD your God will be with you wherever you go." This verse is key in the church's response to fear. God's Word must be central to every message that is spoken. We are not to stray from it in any way. Then we will be equipped with courage to go into the world, set apart and balanced. The bridge between fear and hope is truth, and Jesus is the Truth!

Our spirit yearns for hope. The difficulty lies in the fact that hope cannot be found within ourselves or from the world. The hope we crave can only be found in Jesus. Once we are anchored in Jesus, fear can be minimalized and replaced with the hope we desire. And when we speak truth in love to others, it can bring them into this same revelation of hope in Christ.

If we look to the world for our hope, we will be consistently disappointed. I find it extremely interesting that the exact center of the Bible rests on Psalm 118:8 (NKJV), "It is better to trust in the LORD than to put confidence in man." I absolutely believe God is highlighting this scripture in such a way as to make us aware and attentive. If He is at our core and the center of our lives, we will not give way to worldly extremes that can sink our faith. Nothing the world can say to us or show us can shake our faith. When we are anchored in such a hope, we are powerful and effective in pushing back darkness and radiating the light of Jesus.

One thing is for sure: God is for us (Romans 8:31)! And since he is for us, there is nothing that can stop us, besides ourselves. However, we must decide are we for Him? In this matter, there is no in-between! How do we know where we stand? We must examine our hearts. Scripture tells us to guard our hearts because all things flow from it (Proverbs 4:23). Our heart will reveal what we really stand for. There is a commonly quoted statement; "If you don't know what you stand for, you will fall for anything", which really rings true here.

When it comes to living an effective life that honors God, we must know what God has to say about every issue we face. The only way we know this is by regularly reading scripture. When we read, believe and apply God's Word, then we are set apart.

We are told in scripture multiple times that we are to be set apart from this world and from unbelievers. 1 Peter 2:9 states, "but you are a chosen people, a royal priesthood, a holy nation, God's special possession, that you may declare the praises of him who called you out of darkness into his wonderful light." We have been called out of darkness into the light by God. Therefore, this requires three things from us. First, we should no longer walk in that darkness we were rescued from. Second, we should Praise God for saving us. Finally, we should be guiding others on how to move from darkness to light. This will happen when we are living a life that causes people to realize that we are different (set apart).

This type of living is slowly placing us on the fringe of society in a post-Christian culture. Yet, this is what must happen in order for us to persevere and keep our faith until the end. The world is being shaken and only the remnant will remain. In order to be part of the remnant, we cannot compromise. We must be set apart in every aspect of our lives. J.C Ryle, a well-known Evangelical Bishop who lived in the late 1800's, once said "according to the men of the world, few are going to hell; according to the Bible, few are going to heaven."

If we are true believers then we know that The Word is the ultimate authority.

Yet, another example of imbalance can be seen in our understanding of our relationship with God and how we represent Him to others. We must both love Him and fear Him. Within the church body we can see extremes in some who have fabricated a cotton candy version of God. This preaching focuses consistently on God's love without any additional context. With the popular verse *'God is Love'* as its mantra, the general interpretation of this has come to represent that He also accepts all things, which is simply untrue and dangerous. God cannot accept anything that is in contradiction to His Word, for it is sin. And God is separate from sin.

Love is not a feeling, it is action. God is the source of love. He loves us so much that He gave us His Son to save us from ourselves. It is because of Him and for Him that we learn how to love (1 John 4:19). God's tremendous capacity to love is beyond what we can fathom, yet He is also to be feared. In scripture there are 365 references to not be afraid. However, none of these scriptures are in reference to Him. God alone holds all things in His hand. God is the creator and the judge who we will be accountable to for every thought, word and action we have made. Because of this fact, we should have a reverence, respect and healthy fear of the Lord.

We cannot bring a version of God to others that only focuses on one side or the other. This is a disservice to God and His people.

If the body of Christ is not painting a balanced and accurate picture of God, it is easy to go to an extreme which misrepresents God. This commonly occurs when the church intervenes in worldly matters.

I often pass a church that proudly flies the gay pride flag in front of its building. My heart grieves for that congregation. Because of the ill decisions of those church leaders, that entire church is covered under that banner. The LGBTQ+ agenda is based on pride and we know scripture tells us that pride comes before the fall.

So, how then should this be handled within the church if we say God is love? God does love everyone but, He does not accept everything. The "love" expressed within the LGBTQ+ community directly goes against many scriptures that speak against this type of behavior. It is for this reason God cannot accept it. However, many churches and denominations have embraced this lifestyle choice and have even elevated this community to have a voice within the church and its policies. This puts their entire church under the judgement of God.

This doesn't mean that members of the LGBTQ+ community should be banned from being in church, partaking in worship or being part of fellowship, because God does in fact love them very much. No one should be turned away if they are seeking the Lord. However, they should not have the ability to hold authority or make decisions that impact the church when they are outwardly living against God's laws.

The same would be true for anyone choosing to participate in a lifestyle that is directly divergent from God's Word.

On the other extreme, we have people preaching gloom and damnation for all who have sinned without redemption. God is both merciful and righteous to judge. No one should feel within the church the burning of eternal damnation spurred by the fear of God once they have authentically accepted Christ. Because of what Jesus did on the cross, we are redeemed and restored to God. If a person repents, they should no longer feel condemned. Pointing fingers from the pulpit over sin without preaching about Jesus' love is damaging to the soul. This will separate others further from their relationship with God.

Having a balanced sense of God in terms of love and fear helps us stay strong and grow our faith. On the contrary, an imbalanced picture of God weakens the believer's ability to stand up against the counterfeit versions of love and fear in the secular world. Let's look at examples of how that plays out in recent events.

The "Love is Love" movement within the LGBTQ+ community has caused numerous believers to lose their job, be persecuted or even taken to court for refusing to accept their beliefs about love and relationships between same sex couples. If we say we are followers of Christ, then we must love **ALL** people even if we vastly disagree with them. However, love does not require us to acquiesce to beliefs or become subservient to demands that go against the fiber of our being.

What we are witnessing is that some churches have accepted this lifestyle, even within the highest levels of their ministry, therefore projecting intolerance and hate for those believers who refuse to accept it. Because some churches compromised the Word of God, it weakens the entire body of Christ who is trying to uphold it. The body has not stood united on how to address this issue from a biblical perspective. Therefore, we have been weakened and we are losing this battle. It is for us to be united according to the truth of the Word. We cannot ignore addressing critical issues such as these within the church. Not only must we correct this for the church body, but it sets an example for the rest of society. Here again, we must look to the example from Jesus as he demonstrated truth and grace in handling issues such as these.

Christians who have been standing for God's Word on world issues need back-up. The Church needs to be accountable to scripture and use it as the foundation for all its decisions. Failure to do so renders them ineffective for the Kingdom of God. Once we are a church united, then we will truly see all that we are capable of defeating in this world.

Two additional distractions within the church, which are as dangerous as the imbalances, are known as Progressive Christianity and Legalism. Again, these are two extremes that are looking to divide God's people by taking the focus off of Jesus and turning it towards self. Because these views reflect humans' needs and beliefs about God, they are quickly becoming popular within church settings.

Progressive Christianity teaches that Jesus is one way to God, not *the* way to God. It has taken the benevolence of Jesus' love while denying His deity. Progressive Christianity acknowledges that Jesus was a good human who taught many wonderful lessons. This belief system emphasizes oneness and inclusion around social justice issues. While still maintaining the name of Christianity in its title, it does not hold to any scriptural doctrine that would identify them as Christians. They identify themselves as an 'evolved' faith which focuses on feeling good about being a human in society.

If we examine the issues that Progressive Christianity organizes itself around, they reflect those that are being espoused by the mainstream society. These views are not healthy in the world and they certainly will not be healthy for the church, since it is not based in God's Word.

As the body of Christ, we must be on the lookout for these views within the church and be able to guard against them. As with most of Satan's schemes, big changes do not happen overnight. He prefers the slow and steady approach, eroding away one foundation at a time. Progressive Christian views usually creep in slowly, one issue at a time. It begins with a bending of The Word and continues with a breaking from The Word. This is the very definition of 'progressive'. It is so ironic that they are hiding their agenda in plain sight. Progressive Christianity is on a slow progression to move you away from God.

As for Legalism, it is a belief system that emphasizes works and deeds as the source of righteousness. Rather than the grace offered through faith in Jesus, it puts priority on merit and deserving grace based on what the individual does. Therefore, it denies what Jesus has already done for us to repair our relationship with God. In many ways, this reflects the beliefs of the ancient Jews (Pharisees) who tried to hold to all the laws of Moses, even though in God's eyes, if you broke one law, you broke them all. That is why God sent Jesus to free us from the bondage of the laws. It is impossible for humans to earn their way into God's presence.

The Legalistic view sets believers up to focus on self, rather than Jesus. This view holds the laws and traditions over people and makes them have guilt for not being able to fully obey them. This is a still a predominant mindset within the Catholic Church. There, it is believed that going to church, praying to saints, saying seven Hail Mary's or confessing to a Priest are getting you into a closer presence with God. Some churches have adopted outward symbols and traditions to create the illusion of God's presence, but they are void of meaning. In some cases, these symbols become the things that are worshiped, which gives believers a false sense of security in their relationship with God. God does not have any interest in these outward appearances. He is looking at the heart of the believer. Our job is to be sure that when God searches us, He sees Jesus in our place.

Aside from the life of Jesus, we can gain further insights and guidance from the revelations given to the Seven Churches which are found in the book of Revelation. These churches were imbalanced, and in some cases not distinguishable from the rest of the world in terms of its behaviors. Interesting to note, that the first two churches mentioned, struggle with love and fear, which we just covered extensively.

Not only do these churches represent the church body, but they can also be symbolic archetypes of an individual believer. Within these scriptures about the churches are key insights into understanding the blessing and power that God provides for us when we overcome our weaknesses through Him. Keep in mind, in Revelation we learn that in the end, only two churches remain. As with much of Revelations, it is a foreshadowing and warning to prepare us before Jesus' return. After reading the description of each church, reflect upon which you most identify with. Which do you hope to be more like?

Church of Ephesus, Revelation 2:1-7

It is noted that Ephesus was doing good works and looked like it had it together from the outside, but its heart was in the wrong place. We are told that it had left its first love, Jesus. The weakness of the Church of Ephesus is that it became distracted. So much so, that it abandoned it's passionate pursuit of Christ.

We are told often in scripture to examine our hearts. It is from there that our motivation and intentions flow. Proverbs 4:23 warns, "Above all else, guard your heart, for everything you do flows from it."

Our heart is also the way in which we connect to others and it should always be through love. Jesus commanded in Mark 12:30-31, "Love the Lord your God with all your heart and with all your soul and with all your mind and with all your strength. [31] The second is this: 'Love your neighbor as yourself'. There is no commandment greater than these."

Ephesus needed to correct its path, reform its heart and come back to Jesus. If it can make this correction and overcome its distractions, it will receive the reward of being able to eat from the Tree of Life.

We learn from this warning about the importance of repentance. We can all experience times of weakness in our faith. That is part of being human. What is important is that we recognize it, regroup from it and repent and return to God. This will restore our relationship and faith so we can continue to move forward in strength. Jesus must be our first love.

Church of Smyrna, Revelation 2:8-11

As for the Church of Smyrna, it was gripped with fear. It had been experiencing tribulation and trials of all kinds, even persecutions. Because it had a strong faith, Satan was putting pressure on it and creating tests to break it.

Smyrna was being crushed by the pressures of the day, yet it still remained fruitful for The Kingdom.

Smyrna is exhorted in Revelation to be faithful even to the point of death. It is told to overcome the fear that holds it back from fully living out what God has for it. If it can overcome this fear and persevere, it will receive the Crown of Life and will not be hurt by the second death.

In order to make this a reality, the believers had to die to the flesh in order for fear to not get the best of them. We are told this multiple times in scripture, that to truly live, we must die to self. Romans 8:12-13 states, "Therefore, brothers and sisters, we have an obligation — but it is not to the flesh, to live according to it. [13] For if you live according to the flesh, you will die; but if by the Spirit you put to death the misdeeds of the body, you will live."

The lesson from the message to Smyrna is clear. It is echoed in Galatians 2:20, which says, "I have been crucified with Christ and I no longer live, but Christ lives in me. The life I now live in the body, I live by faith in the Son of God, who loved me and gave himself for me." If we are living for ourselves then that leads us to death anyway. But, if we live for Christ, no matter what happens to our physical bodies, we are guaranteed life eternal. We should not make decisions based on fear.

Church of Pergamos, Revelation 2:12-17

The Church of Pergamos had been faithful in keeping God's name but, it had become too worldly. God acknowledges that Pergamos is in the midst of Satan's realm and is constantly tempted by the outside influences. Pergamos is being influenced by paganism and idolatry and it began to compromise its doctrines.

This is so dangerous in many ways. First, if the church is compromising its doctrines, then it is setting the believers up for judgement. Second, compromising doctrines makes the church weak because it has eroded its foundation of truth. In addition, this sends a mixed message to the rest of the world about who God is.

Pergamos is instructed to rebuke the false doctrines of Balaam and the Nicolaitans and overcome the lascivious lifestyle it had adopted. If it can repent and overcome, its reward will be the ability to eat the hidden manna. It will also receive a white stone with a new name written on it.

The lesson here is that Satan corrupts through compromise. If he cannot get us to fully denounce God, then he creeps in to make us cut corners. Being victorious means being set-apart by God for His purpose. We should be without compromise, distinguished from the rest of the world. This is only possible when we remain true to His Word.

Church of Thyatira, Revelation 2:18-29

Thyatira had been thriving and was able to persevere with love and service. It was doing many good deeds, but it had become corrupt. Thyatira was known for entertaining Jezebel, a false prophet and teacher who was leading believers astray. It was luring believers into idolatry and sexual immorality. It does say that not all of the believers gave into these practices or beliefs. However, we must understand as a church body, if the Church goes down, it tends to take the believers with it. This is when we see believers backsliding in their faith.

Thyatira is warned about the impending judgement that is upon it if it does not rebuke and repent from the spell of Jezebel. The church is told that both it and her will suffer greatly if they do not change their ways. If, however, it can overcome, its reward is to have power over the nations and the ability to rule with an iron rod.

The lesson from Thyatira is to test all spirits. One's down fall can come from just a single voice that is leading you which is not of God. It is important as individuals and as a church body to be discerning and be firm in not allowing ungodly things into our homes and places of worship. We must stand guard as gate keepers looking out for those who seek to destroy the church and defile God's name. Being successful in this gives us power and authority to rule over the nations according to God's Will.

The Church of Sardis, Revelation 3:1-6

Sardis is accused of being dead. While it seems active, the Spirit is not operating in the church. Sardis had become apathetic. It was not supporting the spiritual growth of the believers and it had fallen asleep to its duties. Since the Spirit had gone, Sardis was misguided in its real purpose of meeting the needs of God's people.

Sardis is being called to wake up! It needs to come out of its slumber and be on fire for God. Because of its apathy it became ineffective in making moves for the Kingdom of God. This church needed a revival. If Sardis can overcome, it will be rewarded by being clothed in white raiment and it will not have its name stricken from the Book of Life. Jesus will confess it before His Father and the Angels.

The lesson we learn from Sardis is that we cannot just go through the motions and still call ourselves Christians. With that title comes responsibility. As believers, we must be all-in: mind, body and spirit in serving God. We cannot merely attend church in the physical and leave our hearts at home. Neither can we worship on Sunday and live for ourselves the rest of the week. Carrying on in such a manner will make us ineffective and it also portrays God in the wrong light. We need to be bold in confessing the name of Jesus at all times and all places so that He will confess our names before the Father and the angels.

The Church of Philadelphia, Revelation 3:7-13

The Church of Philadelphia was holding on by a thread. It had been diligent in preaching the Word and upholding God's name, but it had become weak. We are told that Philadelphia had endured with patience.

Philadelphia must not grow weary. It needed to continue to seek opportunities to minister to God's people. Galatians 6:9 speaks of this also, "Let us not become weary in doing good, for at the proper time we will reap a harvest if we do not give up." The way it can accomplish this is through a refreshing of the Holy Spirit and a rededication to praising God for being able to sustain the church until that point. If Philadelphia can overcome and remain strong, it will have the door opened into Heaven. It will be given the name of God and it will be kept from temptation.

The lesson from the Church of Philadelphia is that we do not gain our strength from ourselves or one another. True strength only comes from God and the power of His Holy Spirit. If we are to have the stamina and endurance to finish the race that is before us and be victorious, that will only happen if God is in it. Through God we have the power to do amazing things for the Kingdom. Not only will this bless others, but it is also a blessing to ourselves.

The Church of Laodicea, Revelation 3:14-22

Laodicea possibly receives the harshest warning, yet it may seem that it hasn't done much to deserve it. And that is the point! The church is unaware of just how wretched it is. Laodicea is rich in material things, but poor in spirit. We are told that it is blind and naked spiritually. Because Laodicea is prosperous and in need of nothing, it has become haughty, self-righteous and lukewarm. It had moved forward in a worldly way and left God behind. Its self-sufficiency made it complacent. Laodicea stored up all of the riches for itself and did not use them to serve God or His people.

The warning given to Laodicea states that because it is lukewarm, God will spit it out of His mouth. Laodicea utilized the church to serve its own needs and not God's. God cannot tolerate such behavior. Laodicea needs to fear God and remember to set Him above all things. It should focus on elevating praise, prayer and worship above everything else. If Laodicea is successful and can overcome its depravity, it will be rewarded with the right to be seated with Jesus Christ on His Throne.

The lesson here is to remember that God is the source of all things. Therefore, our blessings should be stewarded in a godly way. We need to avoid arrogance, pride and self-sufficiency which are in opposition to our trust in God and our need for His provision. Also, understand that the moment we take our eyes off God, everything else we do is futile both as individuals and as a church.

We are to utilize these warnings and lessons given to the seven churches to learn what it is God has for us and how we can obtain it. In Revelation 3:19, Jesus says, "Those whom I love I rebuke and discipline. So be earnest and repent." We are not receiving heavy-handed rules, but practical spiritual and life-saving advice from a Father who loves us deeply and wants the best for us. Following God's way will always be best. This surely doesn't mean it will always be easiest.

Jesus did not come to establish a new government, a new religion or a culture. He came as the New Covenant between God and Man. Jesus rebuked those practicing religion without having the Spirit of God. His encounters with the religious leaders at the time resulted in him asking them to question their practices and beliefs. Both the Jews and the pagans where following ideologies that pleased man, tradition and the world, not God.

When the ideologies of a church reflect the outside world, we are in trouble. Jesus spoke of living with the Kingdom mindset and being the body of Christ on earth. We as a church body have fallen far short in this area. The church is supposed to be the representation of the Kingdom on earth, yet the enemy has taken a stronghold within the organized church system. He needs to be cast out from the church to restore power and effectiveness once more. This requires its people, those who God called out and set apart to stand up for the truth of the real Gospel and not compromise anything found in it.

We cannot allow the church to slip into complacency. Walking in love and truth should always be our motivation. It is from these that our true power flows.

For Your Heart

- *Test everything and make sure it is aligned to God's Word. Always side with truth according to His Word.*
- *If you don't know what you stand for you will fall for anything. Stand firm and don't compromise.*
- *Don't depend on experience or tradition. Make your foundation the Word of God.*

For Your Spirit

I thank you God that you have given me Your Word as a foundation and guide for all my decisions. Because of Your Word, I do not have to be tossed about or confused by the circumstances before me, but I can walk boldly knowing that I walk in Your truth. Thank you for sending Jesus, The Word in flesh. I pray for daily renewing of my mind and spirit so I can live my life as a follower of you, grounded in your Word and set apart from this world. In Jesus' name I pray. -Amen

For Your Mind

The Jesus Code- O.S. Hawkins, (2016). Thomas Nelson Publishing. TN

Another Gospel?- Alisa Childers, (2020). Tyndale. IL

Holiness: Its Nature, Hindrances, Difficulties and Roots- J.C. Ryle, (2007). Hendrickson Publishers. MA

Section Two

Refining Ourselves:

Strengthening Our Voice Through Clarity and Commitment

We need to be clear what we believe

and be prepared to share our faith in

an uncompromised way without fear.

Embracing the Power of the Holy Spirit

"The Spirit gives life; the flesh counts for nothing. The words I have spoken to you—they are full of the Spirit and life."

John 6:63

We need to understand that our journey on earth is as a spiritual being having a physical experience, not the other way around. God created us in such a way that we could perceive, believe and receive His Spirit through our free will. It is up to us to embrace the Holy Spirit and let Him work in us. For those who believe, we have been filled with the Spirt of God, the Holy Spirit. This is the fire within us and the power that propels us forward. Without the Holy Spirit, the body is merely a shell, or empty vessel. 1 Corinthians 6:19 reminds us, "Do you not know that your bodies are temples of the Holy Spirit, who is in you, whom you have received from God? You are not your own". Fullness of life comes when we embrace the Holy Spirit and how He works within us and through us.

I have suffered from anemia for a decade. It has made my body weak, and in many ways, it limits me physically from my true potential. We are in a world where so many people are spiritually anemic. Without the Holy Spirit working in us and through us, we are weak, both as individuals and as a church body. Absence of the Holy Spirit causes us to rely on our human capabilities, which are limiting and not effective against the spiritual realm.

The Spirit is so essential to God, He references Him first in Genesis 1, where it tells us that God's Spirit moved over the earth during creation. It is His Spirit that set everything into motion.

Ephesians 6:12 tells us, "For our struggle is not against flesh and blood, but against the rulers, against the authorities, against the powers of this dark world and against the spiritual forces of evil in the heavenly realms." This is so important to understand because it sets us up for the correct type of strategy. We cannot enter the battles we face without the Holy Spirit's guidance.

So many Christians do not know about this power or how to access it. Sadly, it is not addressed in many churches today. Moreover, many churches are not embracing the work of the Holy Spirit within the church itself. The disciples and apostles walked in the Holy Spirit's power and that is how they were effective in accomplishing what Jesus had set before them. We were promised by Jesus that we would have the same access to this power as graciously given to us by The Father. (John 14:26, John 15:26). We are told that we will do great things because we will have God's Spirit within us. (Acts 1:8)

One of the roles of the Holy Spirit is to activate God's Word that is within us. This only works if we first know The Word. Regular reading of scripture strengthens our connection with the Holy Spirit. Encountering God's Word in such a way gives it power, meaning and application in our life.

The Holy Spirit speaks to us and guides our thoughts. We should be developing the ability to sense the Holy Spirit's leading and then act or speak accordingly. While our default response is to respond from the flesh, it is the Spirit that will move us in truth and wisdom. This is a gift that takes a tremendous amount of discipline to refine. We must pray earnestly, commit fully and discern the way of the Spirit in order to have the power Jesus spoke of.

The beauty of developing such a gift is that God promises that for as much as we use it, He will continually renew and refill us. Trusting God to work through us and moving according to the Holy Spirit in both big and small matters builds our faith and allows God to entrust us with even more. Embracing the Holy Spirit gives us supernatural access and power. Our mind cannot comprehend, but our spirit sees into things not of the natural realm, therefore, giving us an advantage over earthly concerns. Once we realize that battles are being fought and won in a different realm, it starts to put things in perspective of what it means to be in God's Kingdom.

In 1 Corinthians 4:19-20, Paul is telling the church that they are not fully realizing what Christ has for them. Paul wants them to learn all that he has and embrace the fullness of the Gospel. He says, "but I will come to you very soon, if the Lord is willing, and then I will find out not only how these arrogant people are talking, but what power they have. [20] For the kingdom of God is not a matter of talk but of power."

As Christians we must not just "talk the talk", but also "walk the walk". We can only do this if we have the Holy Spirit. It is through Him that we live out our fullness in Christ. Jesus told us the Father would be sending us this advocate to comfort, guide and protect us. This is what will set-us apart from the rest of the world.

Refining this power means that we can learn to bend our body to our spirit, rather than the other way around. It is the ability to live abandoned with less of ourselves and more of God. This is the point of true transformation, the realization that we are not bound by this world but given freedom and rest in Jesus. 2 Corinthians 3:17 tells us, "Now the Lord is the Spirit, and where the Spirit of the Lord is, there is freedom."

Other than Jesus Himself, we can learn what complete abandonment is like from Job. After tremendous suffering and loss of every earthly possession, Job was still able to praise God and lean into Him for his strength. Job says in 33:4, "The Spirit of God has made me; the breath of the Almighty gives me life." It was this single factor that allowed Job to carry-on when everything human in him would have given up. The Spirit gives us life. Without Him we are aimless and lifeless.

When we have the Holy Spirit, He gives us spiritual eyes and ears to discern the things happening around us. Then we can act in accordance with The Word. All sin stems from one basic error: we take our eyes off of God and turn them toward ourselves.

Embracing the fact that God's Spirit lives inside of us means we are never alone, and we never have to depend completely on ourselves. The Holy Spirit is our compass to steer us in God's direction. Therefore, we can powerfully choose right over wrong, light over dark.

This does not mean we will always choose correctly, for we know perfection is an impossibility. However, Psalms 119:11 (NKJV) reminds us, "Your word I have hidden in my heart, that I might not sin against you". If we know God's Word and allow The Holy Spirit to guide us at each moment of decision making, we will be powerful to resist temptations and choose what is right more often than not.

For the times in which we fall short and do not choose correctly, The Holy Spirit allows us to sense and discern God's grace. Grace is a wonderful gift given to us by God. It has real practical application in our life and is one of the tools that makes us powerful and effective. There are three forms of grace mentioned in scripture. Each one is available to us and serves a specific purpose. God will freely give grace but we can also ask for it.

The first form of grace is God's granting of special favor in a circumstance. We have all encountered this type of grace at one point or another. It is when we are at the right place at the right time or removed from the wrong place at the just right time. It is also witnessed when good things might seem to just happen without any natural reason or connection.

Sometimes we experience prosperity, success or victory in a situation when the odds may have been against us, or all the factors in the natural do not line up in our favor. These are results of the gift of God's favor and grace. Let us remember to acknowledge God when these instances occur rather than give credit to coincidence or luck.

The second form of grace is when God pours into us in such a way that we reflect His nature and character. Through this grace, others will be able to recognize God in us. This can be manifested in big or small ways. Maybe it is the ability to smile in a tense situation, or the ability to forgive someone who has hurt you. While others might expect worldly reactions to a particular situation, our responses would reflect an alternative way to think, feel and behave. This opens up God's grace to others.

The third form of grace is when God works in us and through us so that we are able to do things that we could not do on our own. This can include having supernatural ability, strength, provision, time or any other characteristic that is not of the flesh. There are tremendous testimonies for this kind of grace. From mothers who have had the ability to lift a car off of their child, addicts being able to quit cold-turkey, or people being healed miraculously, God's grace is in every circumstance. The Holy Spirit will guide us in humility during these circumstances so that we can acknowledge that God was the source of this power and ability, and it was not of our own doing.

While we should definitely be expectant for God's grace, we should also pray for it. God loves to give good gifts to His children. We never have to feel helpless in a situation because God's hand of grace is there for the asking. For whatever type of grace we experience, we should always be thankful. Thank the Holy Spirit that we can recognize and receive it. We can also start praising God now for the grace He will bestow on us.

Jesus often demonstrated all three forms of grace throughout His ministry. God's grace is what will get us through tests and trials. Jesus was also tested during His time on earth. While many flocked to see and hear Him, others accused Him of all sorts of things. He was even accused of being possessed. Because Jesus moved according to the Holy Spirit, others did not know how to handle what they were witnessing because they did not have the Spirit. Jesus warned us about neglecting and speaking against the Holy Spirit. By many theologians, this is considered the only unforgiveable sin. Luke 12:10 says, "And everyone who speaks a word against the Son of Man will be forgiven, but the one who blasphemes against the Holy Spirit will not be forgiven". We are not to deny the work of the Holy Spirit within us or others.

It is certain we will be tested in life and it will be by the power of the Holy Spirit that we are victorious. Jesus continues to say in Luke 12:11-12 (ESV), "And when they bring you before the synagogues and the rulers and the authorities, do not be anxious about how you should defend yourself or what you should say,

[12] for the Holy Spirit will teach you in that very hour what you ought to say." We should approach trials in confidence knowing that the Holy Spirit has been given to us to guide us, even down to what we should say.

Additionally, we must remember that we are not only given the Holy Spirit so we can connect with God, but also so we can connect others to Him. 1 Corinthians 12:7 (NKJV) tells us, "But the manifestation of the Spirit is given to each one for the profit of all." It is when we use the Spirit that God gave us that we glorify Him and show others who He is.

We are told across a multitude of scriptures that a diversity of gifts flow from the Holy Spirit. These gifts take a variety of forms but are all given to us by the grace of God. They are for ourselves and to serve others. 1 Peter 4:10 states, "Each of you should use whatever gift you have received to serve others, as faithful stewards of God's grace in its various forms." These gifts can be broken-down and better understood categorically. They are being presented in the order in which they appear in scripture.

The first type consists of seven attributes found in Isaiah 11:2-3, which demonstrates what we can possess when The Spirit is within us. These represent how the Holy Spirit works through us. These attributes are helpful to the individual and are beneficial for setting us apart from the world.

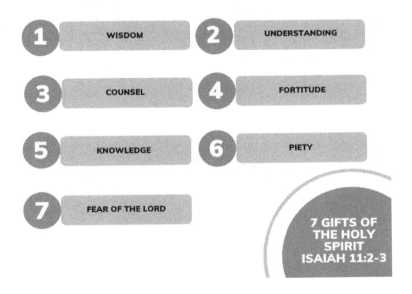

The second type of gifting, mentioned in Romans 12:6, is known as motivational gifts. These seven gifts generally reflect the innate personality of the individual. Everyone has a dominate motivational gift. It is the unique way God has wired us so that we serve the body of Christ. This also tends to lead us in the choices we make in life for our career or other areas of purpose.

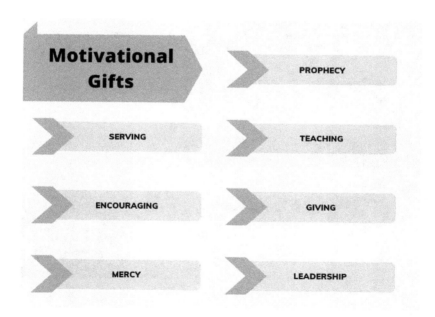

The third type of gifts are introduced to us in 1 Corinthians 12. These nine spiritual gifts reflect the unique abilities bestowed upon us by The Spirit to do the work of The Kingdom and make God known to others. When activated, these gifts are usually signs to a non-believer that the Holy Spirit is at work and that God is who He says He is.

The fourth type of gifting, found in Galatians 5:22-23, is known as the Fruit of The Spirit. These represent the nine fruits we bare when we move in The Spirit. While these benefit the individual, they certainly have impact on others when practiced.

Galatians 5:22-23

Finally, there are the gifts for ministry found in Ephesians 4:11. These five gifts are for unifying and edifying the church. A church functions in fullness when all of these gifts are working for the benefit of each other.

While complete knowledge of the Holy Spirit can be elusive and difficult to comprehend, we must acknowledge that we cannot be effective, powerful, prosperous or victorious without fully embracing Him. This is often difficult for people, particularly because many churches are not preparing believers in such a way. Even the disciples, after seeing Jesus perform miracles, had their doubts and Jesus responded, "The Spirit gives life; the flesh counts for nothing. The words I have spoken to you—they are full of the Spirit and life." The Spirit indeed gives life and fullness of life.

Without acknowledging and moving according to The Holy Spirit as individuals and as a church, we are spiritually dead. Since we know battles are fought and won in the spiritual realm, it is critical that we awaken the spirit inside of us and embrace all that He can give us. God has blessed us through the Holy Spirit with tremendous gifts. Shame on us if we are not using them to their fullness.

For Your Heart

- *We must worship in Spirit and truth.*
- *The power of God is within us through the Holy Spirit.*
- *The Holy Spirit can be renewed in us daily.*

For Your Spirit

Thank you, God for creating me with a spirit that can connect to Your Holy Spirit. Help me to become more aware of how He works in my life. Teach me to develop my dependence on the Holy Spirit so I can walk in spirit and truth daily. Let me embrace the Holy Spirit and receive all the benefits He gives me. In Jesus' name I pray. -Amen

For Your Mind

How to be filled with the Holy Spirit, AW Tozer (2016). Moody's: NY

Embracing the Power of Language

"But I tell you that every careless word that people speak, they shall give an accounting for it in the day of judgement."

Matthew 12:36 (NASB, 1995)

The most commonly committed sins are the ones we commit with our words. Every thoughtless, unkind or blasphemous word that comes out of our mouth is a sin against God. There are just over 100 verses in scripture that reference how we should speak. This is because our words have so much power. Matthew 12:36 states that we will be held accountable for every word we have spoken. The words themselves are not as powerful as the intentions behind them, none the less, we must choose our words wisely, seeking to always represent ourselves and God in a righteous manner.

Language is a mirror for our beliefs and intentions. It reflects what is really in our hearts. Jesus says in Matthew 15:18, "But the things that come out of a person's mouth come from the heart, and these defile them." We need to be more purposeful in aligning our words with our intentions. While language does possess power, the flow of this power can be positive or negative. Words can be sweet like honey (Proverbs 16:24) or deadly like poison (James 3:5). The real power lies in the fact that we have choice on how to use our words.

All of creation was spoken into existence by God (Genesis 1). He created Adam and gave him authority to name everything that was created. Therefore, humans can create and control language. Satan cannot create, so he must manipulate. Satan has been manipulating language since tempting Eve in the Garden of Eden. Furthermore, humans have used language to plan and plot evil and deception for their own gain. So much so, that God had to intervene. In Genesis 11:5-7 we are told, "But the LORD came down to see the city and the tower the people were building. [6] The LORD said, "If as one people speaking the same language they have begun to do this, then nothing they plan to do will be impossible for them. [7] Come, let us go down and confuse their language so they will not understand each other." He confused the language and separated the people so they could not scheme and conspire to do things that would lead to their destruction. Both of these examples illustrate how the intention behind the language use was for evil. Any manipulation of the Word of God is a lie.

Knowing how instrumental language is in all we do should make us mindful of several things. First, we should have awareness for how we speak. This entails two things: what we actually say and how we say it. Before speaking a word, we should reflect on the intention of the utterance. Consider, is this from ourselves or from God? Will what I say produce fruit? Does it serve to build up or tear down? How we respond to these questions gives us insight into the effectiveness of what we say.

Sometimes we might find that not saying anything at all may be the most effective in a given circumstance. Taking a moment between the process of thought and production can help us have better control in this area. We should use God's Word as a filter for how we conduct ourselves. As with all other choices, there are always consequences.

Two biblical examples that illustrate this understanding perfectly can be found in Job and 2nd Kings. In the book of Job, we learn that Job was one of God's most faithful servants. Satan devised a plan to torment Job so that he would curse God and turn away from Him. Satan attacked from every possible angle of Job's life. He killed his family, burned his home, took all his possessions and left him in the depths of despair and loneliness. Yet, Job refused to curse God. As any human would be, he was angry, heartbroken and confused by all that had happened to him. Job even wished to have not been born, but not once did he curse God for his circumstances. Job continued to praise God through it all.

Job realized even in the midst of his dire circumstances, that to speak against God would be a sin. Job makes a better choice and chooses to worship and praise God instead. We are told in Job 1:20-22 after losing all his worldly possessions and his children, "At this, Job got up and tore his robe and shaved his head. Then he fell to the ground in worship [21] and said: "Naked I came from my mother's womb, and naked I will depart.

The LORD gave and the LORD has taken away; may the name of the LORD be praised." ²² In all this, Job did not sin by charging God with wrongdoing."

What a powerful witness for God! This is truly how we impact others. It is when we can face difficult circumstances beyond our comprehension and, rather than demonstrate anger or foul words, we can stop in the moment and praise God with our words because He is still good! This not only demonstrates our faith to others, but it also transforms us in the circumstance. This helps redirect our minds to focus on God rather than our circumstances. It embraces something positive rather than emphasizing what might be negative. This type of self-control is pleasing to God because of the sacrifice it takes to accomplish it. Beyond pleasing God, it also has tremendous benefit for our minds, body and spirit. Not allowing anything profane, evil or blasphemous to come from our mouths will preserve our health and sanity.

The second example comes from 2ⁿᵈ Kings 4. We learn of a Shunammite woman who was kind to Elisha and was without a child. So, God blessed her with a son. Several years later the son dies suddenly. The Shunammite woman does not tell anyone. She immediately goes to find Elisha and while she is rushing off to get help, others are asking her how everything is going. She simply responds, "it is well" (4:23-26). Not once, did she wail, curse, or utter the word death. She had faith in God's protection over her son.

Elisha comes to the house of the woman, as led by the Lord, and stretched himself over the child and the boy came alive. The Shunammite woman fell to her feet and embraced her son.

This woman saw God work before in her life and knew He would do it again. She refused to give credence to the circumstances in the natural world. The Shunammite woman acted in faith, even with her words. She refused to even speak of the death of her son, as to give it any authority. She knew that God would have the final word. This woman could honestly say all was well because she believed it. Her faith was in God, not her circumstances.

An additional detail within this story that is so very interesting is that on the way back to seeing the woman's son, she is instructed by Elisha that if you run into anyone, do not say anything. She was not to speak to or greet anyone along the way, but head straight back to her home (4:29). Sometimes, we are effective when we do not say anything. God often uses silence as powerfully as he uses voice. We must listen to the Spirit and know which to use. Jesus was silent before His accusers because He knew God's Will was for the events to unfold that would lead to His death. If Jesus had spoken up, it could have altered the events and outcomes. Since Jesus was truth, they would have found Him innocent and released Him. Then Jesus would not have been able to fulfill His purpose according to God's Will.

While we are to watch our words, we need also be mindful of what others say. Where is their heart and their intentions? We can ask of them the same questions. Is what they are saying to build-up or tear down? God's Word is life! Anything else is counterfeit.

In current times we are in a war of words. With an increase of social media and the massive amounts of information being spued out daily, it is easy to see how language is used to get people's attention, persuade or even disenfranchise people by using catchy terminology or memes. However, we must be discerning, for we know that not all information is truth. Conspiracy, propaganda and indoctrination run rampant, trying to lure society into submissive thought. We must filter everything we hear through the Word of God.

I once heard a saying that literally changed my entire perspective on everything in life. "Take knowledge from everyone, but only take wisdom from godly people." As an academic, this spoke to me so strongly. Knowledge and wisdom, while similar, are different in purpose. Knowledge is a piece of information, usually perceived as a fact. Wisdom is insight, understanding and application of fundamental truths. So, if I am in need of general information to complete an ordinary task, I would want to find the most knowledgeable and skilled person in that area to guide or mentor me. It is not so vital that they share my faith or beliefs. However, why would I want to seek wisdom from others who have a completely different worldview?

If I need to make critical life decisions, I should not seek advice from those who might act contrary to God's Word. This could have dire consequences to the outcome of my situation. I should aim to always seek godly counsel. Everyone is entitled to their opinion or advice. It is for us to be discerning of the foundation behind it and whether it is sound to follow it or not.

This is spoken of beautifully in Psalm 1:1-6 (NKJV):

Blessed *is* the man
Who walks not in the counsel of the ungodly,
Nor stands in the path of sinners,
Nor sits in the seat of the scornful;
² But his delight *is* in the law of the LORD,
And in His law he meditates day and night.
³ He shall be like a tree
Planted by the rivers of water,
That brings forth its fruit in its season,
Whose leaf also shall not wither;
And whatever he does shall prosper.
⁴ The ungodly *are* not so,
But *are* like the chaff which the wind drives away.
⁵ Therefore the ungodly shall not stand in the judgment,
Nor sinners in the congregation of the righteous.
⁶ For the LORD knows the way of the righteous,
But the way of the ungodly shall perish.

We live in a time when there is more information being disseminated on a daily basis than any other time in history. That does not mean we are more intelligent or have more wisdom than before. It can be argued that it is actually the opposite.

We must consider who or what is the source of the information, if it is accurate, if it is useful and if it is truthful.

We can become enchanted by what people say. No matter how eloquent or powerful the speaker is, we must always hold what they say accountable to God's Word. The world is very skilled at manipulating language to tell half-truths. These pithy phrases sound like they have merit on the surface, yet when you look deeper you discover the sentiment behind them is not anchored in truth. These catchy little phrases infiltrate our mind and mislead our thinking. Further examination reveals that they are really common misconceptions that are dispelled by biblical truth.

The Bible speaks of wisdom and knowledge a multitude of times. Proverbs 4 tells us to get wisdom at all costs. In James 1, we are instructed to ask for wisdom because God gives it to everyone generously. So, why does the world tell us that "ignorance is bliss"? While on the surface, this may ring true, since not knowing certain things helps us not be mindful or worried about it, therefore bringing a perception of peace or happiness. In actuality, ignorance is bondage. It allows for suppression and delusion, keeping people trapped under a spell of ungodly authority.

Scripture tells us something contrary to this cliche. In Hosea 4:6 (NKJV) it states, "My people are destroyed for lack of knowledge. Because you have rejected knowledge, I also will reject you from being priest for Me;

Because you have forgotten the law of your God, I also will forget your children." Our minds are protected when we have God's wisdom and knowledge (His law). It helps us to address the world's issues from a godly perspective. This gives us an advantage over others who only know what the world tells them. 1 Corinthians 3:18-19 states, "Do not deceive yourselves. If any of you think you are wise by the standards of this age, you should become "fools" so that you may become wise. [19] For the wisdom of this world is foolishness in God's sight. As it is written: "He catches the wise in their craftiness"

Another common half-truth is "God won't give you more than you can handle." The problem here is that the most important part of this saying has been left out. God never makes the promise that we won't experience difficult things or that we can handle everything that comes our way. However, He does promise that He will always be with us. Without Him, there will definitely be things we cannot handle, and they just might be the cause or our demise. Our only hope against the difficulties in this life is Jesus. We must be careful to not believe in this saying in part, but fully realize that God must be in it if we are to handle it. Otherwise, we fall victim to self-sufficiency and pride.

And yet another half-truth, "when there is a will there is a way". Sure, we are resourceful and can work our way around a number of situations, but at what expense? Just as with the previous saying, if we are leaning on our own will, we should proceed with caution.

This is equivalent to "the ends justify the means." Are we willing to sacrifice everything in this world and possibly eternity to have things turn out the way we see fit? Leaning on God's Will is the better choice. He will be able to lead us in the best outcomes for our own sake.

Along with these half-truths come, what I call, secularisms. These are mantras or mottos that the world uses to cheer on its agenda. We are in great danger of falling prey to these secularisms because we want to appear that we still fit-in and are part of the crowd. We may start to repeat these as a way to remain relevant, but before you know it, we might also be living them out. These sayings can create a slippery slope in our thinking. We have all heard them and have maybe even used them. Taking inventory of our language can help us see what we think and believe on the inside. One thing these secularisms have in common is that they are focused on self. Not surprising after what was addressed in a previous chapter about society's fixation on self. The prolific use of these phrases are a window to our intentions.

"You only live once, (YOLO) right? So, why shouldn't we be able to justify any behavior or activity we want? We are only going to get this one life, so we should live it to the fullest to please ourselves." While it is true that life is short, we still want our time on earth to be meaningful and pleasing to God. This saying leads to a self-serving attitude and carte blanche behavior, possibly without thought to consequences to ourselves, others or eternity.

"You do you." This is used to accept behavior that we might feel is straying, without putting that person down. It gives us the ability to ignore the behavior and the consequences and check-out of any type of accountability. Basically, it translates to 'I won't tell you how to live and you shouldn't involve yourself in what I do either.' Again, this is self-serving and a cop-out of responsibility. If we truly love and care for others, our response should be more like, 'Have you considered this choice/behavior and how God sees it?' 'Maybe you can pray about it first'.

"Live your truth." First of all, it is impossible for each person to have their own version of truth. There is absolute truth and then there are shades of deceit. While we may have different perspectives, there can only be one truth. Our absolute truth should be the Word of God. We cannot justify living out anything that is not in alignment with God's Word. Supporting the 'live your truth' mindset is so misleading. Deception only has one destination: a dead end.

"You got this." No, you actually don't. No one in history has! If it was not for the grace of God working for us in our lives, we could not get through anything. Realizing our strength comes from Him and not ourselves is so critical to our success in everything. We should not be patting ourselves on the back or encouraging others to be self-sufficient in critical life areas. If we love them, we should tell them to completely empty themselves, so God can get to work.

Another common phrase is "just have faith." My question is, faith in what? Even an atheist has faith; faith in themselves. They are so self-confident they do not need to bother with any higher authority. If we are looking toward faith in anything other than Jesus, we will be sadly disappointed. People throw around this saying so much that it has lost all of its spiritual intention. Again, it is not so much of the words we speak, but the meaning behind it. If one believes that faith in anything of this world is going to save them, my heart genuinely grieves for them.

We must guard against making the worlds language become our language. We are experiencing, in part, these issues related to language so dramatically because of the increase in social media usage. However, it is more a result of the lack of accountability. People are not always held to what they say. Society has made it very easy to inhabit the airwaves for a moment, say what you feel and then walk away with no consequence. Unless you try to speak the truth, that is another story. We have become accustomed to just posting something in the moment without giving it much thought.

We should reflect upon if we would say the same thing to a person face-to-face. Would we be willing to put our money and resources behind what we say? Would we be willing to die for that belief? Do our words reflect life, truth, integrity and compassion? This is what we should fill our speech with. For it is from our words that we will eat its fruits.

We are told in Proverbs 18:20-21 "From the fruit of their mouth a person's stomach is filled; with the harvest of their lips they are satisfied. The tongue has the power of life and death, and those who love it will eat its fruit."

While we may possess the Word of God, which is truth, we must be effective in how we communicate that with others. Jesus was *the* example for speaking the truth in love. Jesus spoke with passion, power and compassion (Ephesians 4:15). Paul reminds us that our charge is to make an effort to interact with each other with grace so we are able to speak in such a way that others will listen and want to hear the good news. He says in Ephesians 4:29 (NASB, 1995), "Let no unwholesome word proceed from your mouth, but only such a word as is good for edification according to the need of the moment, so that it will give grace to those who hear." He reminds us again in Colossians 4:6 (NASB, 1995), "Let your speech always be with grace, as though seasoned with salt, so that you will know how you should respond to each person."

So, being able to genuinely and consistently speak in such a way requires conscious choice and repeated practice. This is not a default setting for the flesh. If we want to win people for Jesus, our words need to speak truth in love all the time. This is not just in our direct interactions, but in every circumstance we encounter, especially to those who do not have kind words for us.

Power does not always have to come with force. One thing that I have found particularly effective is making sure to interact with people in the kindest manner possible. Even if it is under difficult or unpleasant circumstances, stepping forward in a demeanor and words that are pleasing to God is also pleasing to people. For example, if I am at the store or on the phone with customer service, regardless if I get my situation resolved, I try to always end the conversation with thank you and have a blessed day. There is an immediate change of the environment when we respond in such a way. It often catches people off guard and makes them notice that you are different. It also cleanses our mind so we do not take any negative feelings that may have built up from that exchange into our next interaction.

Based on scripture, every encounter is an opportunity to share Jesus, both directly through the Gospel or indirectly through our character. People are always watching and listening to how we speak and respond. We discussed in an earlier chapter about how the world views many Christians as hypocrites. This is partially due to how we speak. James 1:26 (NLT) tells us, "If you claim to be religious but don't control your tongue, you are fooling yourself, and your religion is worthless." Others will not listen to or take us seriously if we are not above reproach with our words. Let's be like Job and sin not with our tongue.

Choosing our words carefully is not just for the benefit of others, but for ourselves as well. Jesus tells us in Matthew 12:37 (NKJV), "For by your words you will be justified, and by your words you will be condemned." We are setting a path for ourselves by how we speak. If our words are aligned with God's Word then our path is promising.

This is not just in a figurative sense but literal as well. Negative words harbor negative energy, attract negative spirits and can even lead to physical stress and disease. None of which equals a positive outcome. 1 Peter 3:10 (NLT) says, "If you want to enjoy life and see many happy days, keep your tongue from speaking evil and your lips from telling lies." Proverbs 16:24 (ESV) says, "Gracious words are like a honeycomb, sweetness to the soul and health to the body." Finally Proverbs 15:4 (ESV) tells us, "a gentle tongue is a tree of life, but perverseness in it breaks the spirit."

So, choose to speak life over yourself and those you love. Take scriptures and turn them into pep-talks when you hit a rough patch. Infuse God's Word into your prayers. Use the power of God's Word to ignite the Holy Spirit to do great things in and through you. Encourage others with the truth of God's Word. Enjoy and share the fruits of positive and powerful words.

For Your Heart

- *Language is powerful so use it wisely.*
- *Language is easily manipulated so be discerning.*
- *We must represent Jesus in how we speak.*

For Your Spirit

Thank you God that you have created me with free will to love and serve you. Please help to guard my heart and mind against the deceptions of the day. Give me the words to speak grace, truth and love in all circumstances. Let me be identified as your follower by how I interact with others. In Jesus' name I pray. -Amen

For Your Mind

Tell It Slant- A Conversation on the Language of Jesus in His Stories and Prayers, Eugene H. Peterson (2008). Eerdmans Publishing. MI

The Language Police-How Pressure Groups Restrict What Students Learn, Diane Ravitch (2003). Vintage Books. NY

Embracing the Power of Testimony

"And I tell you, everyone who acknowledges me before men, the Son of Man also will acknowledge before the angels of God, ⁹ but the one who denies me before men will be denied before the angels of God."

Luke 12:8-9 (ESV)

Everyone reading this has been tested in life. Being that you are still here, you can testify that you made it out the other side by the grace of God. This is our testimony. Because we have a relationship with a living and loving God, it should be our desire to share this testimony with anyone who will listen, and even those who are hesitant. It just might save someone's life, literally and spiritually.

Our best testimony is how we live our lives and carry ourselves in word and deed. Just as each one of us was created uniquely by God, He has gifted each of us with a powerful and unique testimony. Our testimony is not just for the benefit of ourselves, but for others. If we have experienced and witnessed God personally work in our lives, we cannot keep quiet. Jesus says in Luke that we should be speaking His name in public, telling and confessing all He has done for us.

There is a movement to silence voices like ours, therefore others may not often get to hear about God in such a personal or powerful way. Unbelievably, some still have yet to hear anything about Jesus.

This therefore means it becomes an obligation as a Christian to let others know about Him. Every encounter is an opportunity to speak about Jesus. We do not need a ministry, a stage or a platform to share Jesus. It can happen in the grocery store aisle, the doctor's office waiting room, outside school while waiting to pick up your child, etc. There are no boundaries that Jesus cannot cross.

The world is crying out. It is in desperate need of the peace and comfort that only Jesus can give, yet so many still do not know Him. Imagine how important it is for someone who is struggling to hear about the hope Jesus can offer. You do not need a script or a polished speech. You need compassion, truth and your testimony. Think about making a personal connection first and move in an authentic conversation before jumping in with Jesus. Keep in mind, there will be opposition. Not from the person you are speaking to necessarily, but from Satan. The enemy's only job is to separate people from God. Surely, he does not want you telling others of how great He is.

If you sense this is the case, take a moment and pray. Ask the Holy Spirit to guide you in what to say and to give you the courage to face the opposition. Don't miss an opportunity to be part of the reason someone considers Jesus. Don't shrink back in fear. Go boldly and proclaim His name.

I am always happy to share my testimony with everyone and anyone who listens. That is because it so clearly demonstrates how the Living God is at work within my life. I have seen God move countless times on my behalf in ways that simply cannot be explained in the natural. Although it might be my story, it is always for His glory. Seeing God's love and power in such a personal way is something that cannot be hidden. It must be proclaimed so that others get to know the relational God.

The power of a testimony lies in one important detail, which is, it is only when we have come to the end of ourselves (and this world) that we see God show up BIG! Our flesh has us holding on to every thread of control in a futile manner to fix our own situations. However, it is only when we are barely hanging on by a thread that God has the room to do what He does. Being aware of this fact and conveying it to others can have real impact. Those who are in desperation, are lonely, feel hopeless or are depressed need to know they can let go and let God in. Someone is waiting to hear that from you. They are waiting for someone to take over the burden they have been bearing. They are waiting for that hope that has eluded them from everywhere else. Consider this: sharing Jesus with someone can literally save a life, both in the present and for eternity. That is truly amazing!

The pressure from the world is like living in a powder keg. Pressures from society are making people "essed" to death. They are in danger of becoming stressed, obsessed, depressed, possessed, and oppressed.

But with Jesus we are set free from all of these. Jesus offers us a better way. His yoke is light (Matthew 11:28-30). This is surely something we should be sharing with everyone we meet. Nothing this world has to offer can do what Jesus has already done and will continue to do for us. However, people cannot choose Jesus if they do not know He exists and is real. This is why God has called us to share our testimony, to make Him known to others.

Romans 10:17 tells us, "Consequently, faith comes from hearing the message, and the message is heard through the word about Christ." When we utter something, it brings validity to it. It is no longer just something in our head, it is now part of the environment. It becomes tangible and hearing it reinforces it in our mind. So, when we speak God's Word and share our testimony, it not only builds our faith, but edifies others and increases their faith as well.

Just like love, faith is not passive. It requires action. If we say we have faith in God, in what ways do we show and move in that faith? Faith is only powerful when it is applied. Taking a step in faith starts with acknowledging God is at the center of all things. We strengthen this connection every time we share Him with others. It reminds us just how much He is doing within our lives. It reinforces our beliefs and helps us trust that God will continue to work in our lives.

Not every act of faith needs to be huge. We should never underestimate the power of one person's witness. In 2009, during the College Football National Championship, Tim Tebow wore John 3:16 on his black undereye strips. It is estimated that 90 million people searched that verse on Google and it was the number one trending item on social media.[4] Coincidentally (Yes it was God!), his team won the game. From one person who stepped out in faith, millions of people had the opportunity to find Jesus. Take every opportunity to step out in faith and proclaim His name.

Testimonies have been powerful tools for The Kingdom, bringing many people to Christ. In particular, there is tremendous power in conversion stories. Hearing how someone who did not know Christ was called out of the darkness is extremely insightful in learning how God reaches people at an individual level. Sometimes it happens when someone is actively seeking answers. For some it happens in dreams and for others it may seem like a small coincidence, but they learn it was all God. No matter the details of the encounter, the power came from the Holy Spirit revealing truth to that person in the moment. The Holy Spirit was witnessing to the truth of Jesus Christ. What could be more authentic than your own personal encounter with Jesus and the Holy Spirit?

---

[4] https://fanbuzz.com/college-football/sec/florida/tim-tebow-john-316/

If you struggle with confidence in sharing your testimony, find people who have shared theirs with powerful impact. Be encouraged by their message and look at the way in which they presented it. There are some powerful examples listed in the end of this chapter to use as a starting point. In many cases, the courage it took for some to share their story meant that they had to give up everything. For example, in the case of Muslim conversions, often they are disowned by their families and could even suffer death. Yet, the force within them was so great to still share what God had revealed to them, they risked it all.

Be bold and pray that God will give you opportunities to share your testimony. Ask the Holy Spirit to guide your words and pray the blood of Jesus over you for protection from persecution. That is all you need to do to get started.

In the early church days of Acts, the disciples counted on their testimony to spread the good news because they did not have scriptures yet. We learn in Acts 14:3 (NASB, 1995), "Therefore they spent a long time there speaking boldly with reliance upon the Lord, who was testifying to the word of His grace, granting that signs and wonders be done by their hands." It was this intimate, personal contact of meeting people in the streets, where they were, with the good news that spread the joy of Christ. We have moved so far away from this example because we have left the job of witnessing primarily to The Church.

Unfortunately, religion has gotten in the way of the message in most churches and the personal connection has been lost.

We cannot only speak of what Jesus has done on Sunday mornings. Jesus commissioned us "to go out into the whole world and preach the Gospel to all of creation" (Mark 16:15). The two keys to this scripture is 1) Jesus said "go-out", which means we are not waiting for someone to 'come' and ask. We must go-out in faith and approach others. This is a 24/7 commission, not a part-time possibility. Secondly, Jesus said "all-creation". That means we should not fear those who might reject us because they believe something different from us. We are not limited to 'preaching to the choir'. Our mission field is everyone we encounter.

Again, Acts 28:31 (NASB) encourages us in this, saying they were "preaching the kingdom of God and teaching concerning the Lord Jesus Christ with all openness, unhindered." So let's be bold, recommit to our commission from the Lord and acknowledge His name before men so He will acknowledge our name before the Father.

For Your Heart

- *We have a testimony because we have a relationship with the Living God.*
- *How we live our life is our greatest testimony.*
- *Our testimony can save someone else.*

For Your Spirit

God, I thank you that even in the trials, there is a reason to praise you. Let my life magnify your gloriousness. Let my test become my testimony so that others will see you in me. I pray for courage to speak boldly of all you have done for me. In Jesus' name I pray. -Amen

For Your Mind

Seeking Allah Finding Jesus: A Devout Muslim Encounters Christianity, Nabeel Qureshi (2014) Zondervan Books. MI.

Hiding in the Light, Rifqa Bary (2015) Waterbrook Press. CO.

Losing My Voice to Find It: How A Rock Star Discovered His Greatest Purpose, Mark Stuart (2019) Thomas Nelson Publishing. TN.

Section Three

Preparing Ourselves:

Tools for Standing Firm

We need to not shrink back or be fearful because we are equipped by God to handle what is before us.

Putting On the Armor of God

"Finally, be strong in the Lord and in his mighty power. [11] Put on the full armor of God, so that you can take your stand against the devil's schemes."

Ephesians 6:10-11

If we live out our beliefs as described in this book thus far, there will no doubt be opposition and resistance from the enemy. We will not be able to overcome this opposition if we do not willfully and strategically put on the full armor of God daily. God has given us all the spiritual tools that we need. We must be sure we know how to access them and apply them.

We will look at all facets of what this entails with a specific emphasis on prayer. As we have seen spiritual warfare increase in these days, many Christians are more aware of lessons about the armor of God. Yet, are they really being applied as if our life depends on it, because it in fact does.

The entire book of Ephesians is dedicated to understanding the power and identity we have in Christ. In Ephesians 6, we learn how to defend ourselves against Satan who is trying to take away everything that Jesus has placed in our hands, including our lives. Throughout this book we have explored God's character, Jesus as our savior and role model and how to embrace the Holy Spirit.

While it is critically important to know as much as we can about those who are on our side, it is also important to know our enemy.

Satan's only agenda is to separate us from God. Everything he does in our life is for that purpose. Scripture tells us that he comes to steal, kill and destroy (John 10:10). We also know It is impossible for him to tell the truth (John 8:44). The good news is we know that he has been crushed by Jesus, who was victorious (1 John 3:8). While Satan does possess power, he has no authority unless we give it to him.

Satan will not announce himself and let you know that he is there to destroy your life. He is going to slip in unannounced, but he was not uninvited. Every aspect of our life that is not in alignment with God is a crack and an opportunity for him to take up ground in our life. The following story illustrates this point perfectly.

On a recent trip to Haiti, I heard a Haitian pastor illustrate to his congregation the need for total commitment to Christ. His parable:

A certain man wanted to sell his house for $2,000. Another man wanted very badly to buy it, but because he was poor, he couldn't afford the full price. After much bargaining, the owner agreed to sell the house for half the original price with just one stipulation: he would retain ownership of one small nail protruding from just over the door.

After several years, the original owner wanted the house back, but the new owner was unwilling to sell. So, the first owner went out, found the carcass of a dead dog, and hung it from the single nail he still owned. Soon the house became unlivable, and the family was forced to sell the house to the owner of the nail.

The Haitian pastor's conclusion: "If we leave the Devil with even one small peg in our life, he will return to hang his rotting garbage on it, making it unfit for Christ's habitation." - Dale A. Hays

Leadership, Vol X, #3 (Summer, 1989), p. 35[5]

We must do everything we can to make it clear that Satan is not welcome in our life, our home or our children's lives. We must guard each of these aspects of our life with the blood of Jesus and the full arsenal of weapons God has bestowed upon us. We can defend ourselves against Satan's schemes and tricks because we know how he operates.

It is impossible to make it out of this life without encountering Satan, since this world belongs to him. Evil will always be a reality until the final day when Jesus returns. As we see evil increase around us in these times, we may want to respond in fear.

---

[5] https://bible.org/illustration/one-nail

However, one strategy that is helpful for overcoming this is to not focus on what Satan is doing, but to look at what God is doing and what Jesus has already done.

Satan knows God's plan for us and Satan knows that he is defeated. Satan is well aware that his time is getting shorter, so he is working harder to take as many people down with him as possible. When there is a big movement of evil, that is in response to a big movement of God and His Kingdom. This is something to be hopeful about rather than fear. Let's decide to praise God for how He is building, rather than focusing at what Satan is trying to tear down.

In between the now and the final victory, it is for us to be strategic and consistent in how to address evil. Remembering to apply the armor of God daily is the first step. God has positioned us so that we can stand against Satan with practical tools for defense. In addition, He has given us one tool that is for offense: The Word. Each tool in the armor serves a specific purpose and can work alone, but when used in combination, they are extremely powerful in overcoming the battle.

The first piece of armor mentioned in Ephesians 6:14 is the belt of truth. Since the belt is fastened around our waist, it focuses on our center. Truth must be the center of all of our thoughts and actions. Remember, the truth is not just The Word of God, but it is Jesus himself, The Living Word. We can rebuke the schemes of the enemy with just the name of Jesus. Call out His name and watch the enemy flee.

Make a firm decision to trust in Jesus and the truth of God's Word, so you can stand against the lies of this world.

The second piece of armor, also in Ephesians 6:14, is the breastplate of righteousness. Righteousness is living a life that is aligned to God's Word. If we are protecting ourselves with right living, we are already setting ourselves in strength because we know that God is with us. From this righteousness we can respond with boldness and without fear.

Next are the shoes of The Gospel of Peace, found in Ephesians 6:15. When we have our shoes on, we are ready to run. We must be prepared at all times to speak and act on behalf of the good news of Christ. Peace comes from living out this good news. Walking in this peace is a defensive mechanism to de-escalate situations because we are walking in Christ.

Ephesians 6:16 tells us to take up the shield of faith. Our faith protects from the fiery darts of the enemy. Because we have an anchor in our faith, the enemy cannot throw us off-course as easily. This shield of faith allows us to trust God rather than rely on our own strength. When we have complete trust in God, we are protected and secured from the things in this world. God is our shield and our ever-present help in times of trouble (Psalm 46:1).

We also have access to the helmet of salvation in Ephesians 6:17. The helmet protects our minds from lies and deception. Remember, the enemy wants to separate us from God, so he tells us all kinds of things. But our salvation that comes from accepting Jesus is secured.

We cannot lose it; we can only give it away. Protecting our minds from the enemy's manipulation is so vital. Do not give your mind over to him. Stay focused on Jesus.

Finally, we are given the sword of the Spirit, which is the only offensive weapon in the armor. The sword of the Spirit is the Word of God. The Word is our power. The spoken Word of God has authority and does not return void (Isaiah 55:11). The Word is alive and sharper than a double-edged sword (Hebrews 4:12). The Spirit will guide us in what to say in difficult circumstances and it will always align with God's Word.

The enemy will try to attack us from every direction. Making sure we remind ourselves that God has equipped us to be victorious takes daily renewal. These are not tools we put in a closet to get dusty. We must keep them handy for daily use and remember to use them. We are only powerful and effective when we can stand against the enemy's schemes. The armor of God prepares us for that. When we are victorious in our battles, then we can lend our strength to others.

In Luke 22:31-32, Jesus warns Simon to watch out for Satan because he wants to destroy him. But Jesus responds that He prayed for Simon's faith to increase to withstand this attack. Jesus also tells Simon that when he has stood against the attack, to go back and strengthen others.

Prayer is pivotal in accessing and rightly using the tools that God has given us. We cannot underestimate the power of prayer.

You might very well be reading this because someone long ago prayed for you to know Jesus. We do not always see the outcome of our prayers or even realize when they are answered. Prayer is communication with the magnificent creator of the universe, our all-loving Abba, who knows every hair on our head. There is nothing more powerful than that.

Prayer should be our first line of defense. Often, we resort to prayer only after we have tried everything else. If we changed nothing else in our life but this one thing, we would see a huge shift by consistently going to God first rather than looking to ourselves. Our mindset is so counter-productive to our own well-being. Sometimes we are our worst enemy. Prayer will focus us, empower us and infill us with God's presence and wisdom. Through prayer we have access to God in indescribable ways.

There is often hesitation, misunderstanding and self-conscious attitudes when it comes to prayer. Partly, this is because prayer is not something that we are directly trained for during our life. Also, most churches do not regularly lead people in understanding prayer. For many believers, prayer may just be something repeated out of reverence without any meaning.

Prayer is essential and extremely meaningful. One of the schemes of the enemy is to intercept any communication between us and God. We may have feelings of anxiety, doubt or hesitation with prayer because the enemy has manipulated us into thinking it is a futile fantasy to think we can communicate with God.

Satan knows that prayer is powerful and effective and it avails much (James 5:16). He wants to distract us from doing it. Satan is good at this too. He will make us feel unworthy, make us too tired, keep us busy or make us doubt that prayer works, all to keep us from doing it.

How can our one prayer have so much impact? First, we are not praying alone. We are told that the Holy Spirit prays with us (Romans 8:26). Also, when we pray according to God's Will, Jesus is also interceding for us and He has direct access to the Father, so our requests are magnified. In addition, we can unite our prayers with others. When we pray in agreement for big concerns, it amplifies and brings God's Will to earth. If you have ever seen ants at work, you understand this concept. Several ants working together can carry out a task 10-times bigger than themselves. We are strong within ourselves because of God, but when we are working and praying together, we are unstoppable. Satan fears this more than anything. If we come in agreement with God through prayer, Satan knows his scheme will not see the light of day.

Prayer is not passive, it is active. There is power in prayer because our spirit is in agreement with the confessions of our words. This is why prayer should be authentic and from the heart, not rote and scripted. We cannot just consider how our prayer looks in an earthly manner, we need to realize that it has impact in the heavenly realms as well. Our prayer will loose or bind things on earth and in heaven.

Another important thing about prayer is that it is a two-way street. While God will not necessarily give an audible response, He will move your mind and spirit to communicate in return. We need to have the eyes and ears of our spirit open and receptive to Him.

While there is no 'formula' for it, there are things we know about prayer because scripture refers to it often. First using Jesus as our example, He prioritized prayer. He did not do anything without communicating with God first.

Jesus gives us a model prayer in Matthew 6:9-13, what has come to be known as The Lord's Prayer. While we can and should repeat this prayer, it is also a guideline for how to approach God in communication. First is to acknowledge who God is and give Him praise (Our Father who art in heaven, hallowed be thy name). Second is to be open to and responding according to God's Will (thy Kingdom come, thy Will be done on earth as it is in heaven). Then we can make our requests known to Him (Give us this day our daily bread and forgive our sins as we forgive those who sin against us). Finally, we can ask God to strengthen and protect us for the battles ahead (lead us not into temptation and delivers us from evil). This prayer is like another piece of armor we can put on each day to cover all our bases. However, it should not just become a rote memorization that rolls off of our tongue, but rather a meditation that flows from our heart as we connect and communicate with our Father.

There are some additional specifics about prayer found in other scripture verses that are helpful for developing an effective prayer life. We are told in 1 Thessalonians 5:16-18 (ESV), "Rejoice always, [17] pray without ceasing, [18] give thanks in all circumstances; for this is the will of God in Christ Jesus for you." So, we know we should be praying continually and at all times. That makes us aware that there is no set or 'proper' time. God hears us whenever and wherever we pray. Often my most effective prayers are when I stop in the moment because I felt led to pray. There is great momentum behind a prayer like that.

These verses also clue us in, that part of the purpose of prayer is gratitude. Before we request anything, we should be praising and thanking God for all He has already done. Sometimes we want to just jump right in with the pressing need of the moment. Better yet, establishing a habit of just praying to praise and thank without a request. This will mature our spirit and give us even more strength.

Prayer doesn't change God's mind, it changes ours. Prayer should be transforming our mind, aligning it more closely to His. Since we have a relational God, communication is essential in a relationship, so prayer is that communication. Through prayer we can communicate with Him intimately and fully. There is nothing that surprises God, but the fact that we took time to tell Him shows that we love Him, trust Him and want Him at the center of our life.

Being in close communication with God has tremendous impact because it puts us in a position of wisdom, safety and favor. These create a hedge of protection around us when we enter into a battle.

When we don't know what to pray, we can pray scriptures. Find the verse that speaks to the circumstances before you and speak God's sweet and powerful words out in the open. Claim the words of scripture over your circumstances and ask God to work faithfully according to what His Word says.

Philippians 4:6 tells us, "Do not be anxious about anything, but in every situation, by prayer and petition, with thanksgiving, present your requests to God." This verse reveals that prayer is the answer to worry. We should not be anxious about anything because our trust is in God who loves us. We can tell God what is on our heart and what we need. God listens when we speak to Him and He wants good things for us. Several scriptures tell us that God is close to those that call on Him. We can count on His presence and this should give us great peace and comfort during our times of stress.

Hebrews 4:16 reminds us to go to God in confidence; "Let us then approach God's throne of grace with confidence, so that we may receive mercy and find grace to help us in our time of need." There should never be a time when we enter a battle alone. God goes before us if we call on Him. We will receive grace, mercy and strength through prayer.

Scripture also tells us that we should not doubt when we pray (1 John 5:15, Matthew 21:22). God desires for us to ask, seek and knock. We need to believe that He will answer when we do.

Knowing we can call upon God in such an immediate and intimate way should ground us in understanding that we have access to heaven and the blessings contained within it. This puts us in a position of strength, power and authority when facing the circumstances of this world. Praying and putting on the armor of God daily will set us apart and protect us from anything that the enemy has planned for us. Then we can truly say that there is no weapon that is formed against us that can prosper, because we are covered by the mighty power of the Almighty God (Isaiah 54:17).

For Your Heart

- *We are in a battle not against flesh and blood, but with spirits.*
- *We have been equipped with tools to overcome and be victorious in these battles.*
- *Our tools need to be sharpened each day.*

For Your Spirit

Thank you, God that you have equipped me with the tools I need for battle. I thank you for the victories I can win through you. I pray for strength in my spirit to stand firm when I am up against the enemy. I ask for a daily renewal of faith to press-on forward. In Jesus' name I pray.

- Amen

For Your Mind

Becoming A Prayer Warrior- A Guide to Effective and Powerful Prayer, Elizabeth Alves (1998) Regal Books. CA.

Defending the Faith- Apologetics

"...but in your hearts honor Christ the Lord as holy, always being prepared to make a defense to anyone who asks you for a reason for the hope that is in you; yet do it with gentleness and respect."

1 Peter 3:15 (ESV)

Defending the faith is not about who is louder in the debate. It is not about who "wins". It is about being effective in moving the heart of the non-believer and planting a seed in their mind. 1st Peter is the definition of apologetics. It is being able to state and defend your faith in such a way that it is powerful, logical and presented with gentleness and respect.

We are now in a time that was prophesied in the early church days. A time when people will not listen to reason and have turned from God's Word. Paul charges us in 2 Timothy 4:2-5, "Preach the word; be prepared in season and out of season; correct, rebuke and encourage—with great patience and careful instruction. [3] For the time will come when people will not put up with sound doctrine. Instead, to suit their own desires, they will gather around them a great number of teachers to say what their itching ears want to hear. [4] They will turn their ears away from the truth and turn aside to myths.

[5] But you, keep your head in all situations, endure hardship, do the work of an evangelist, discharge all the duties of your ministry." We need to be the anchored in our faith and keep moving forward in truth.

We are also reminded in Colossians 4:5 to "be wise in the way you act toward outsiders; make the most of every opportunity." Being prepared as described in these verses means knowing the Word of God, understanding the doctrines of belief and having courage to speak in defense of them. Doing so will help us bring to light any false ideologies that threaten to take over the minds of the church and the culture. This chapter will explore how to prepare ourselves to make this defense and do so in a God-honoring way. Once again, we will refer to Jesus as our example.

Most often, it is not so much what we say, but how we say it that impacts people. It was once said that people may forget what you said or did, but they won't forget how you made them feel. God came down to earth in human form through Jesus to personally deliver salvation to us. Since we are created by a relational God, He understands how important the human connection is. We should consider this when we are sharing Jesus with others.

While we do want to present the truth in a logical and rational way, leading with our heart and a personal connection is going to be what will get people's attention. This is best accomplished when we can open a conversation through questioning.

Questions are a powerful way to get others to really consider what it is that they believe and it brings awareness to their own thoughts. Jesus used this technique often. Many times, Jesus replied to a question asked of Him, with a question in return. For example, in Matthew 16:13, Jesus asks Simon Peter, "who do you say I am?" This gives an opportunity for others to speak first and gives you a window into their thinking based on their response. It is from their response that you can build your case.

We must always be prepared to share the Gospel in a manner that is respectful, graceful and joyful. Proverbs 15:1 states, "A gentle answer turns away wrath, but a harsh word stirs up anger." We do not want to come across as arrogant or abrasive. Speaking the truth in love is what is needed. Remember that no one is keeping points and our goal is to change people's minds.

When sharing a message, one must consider their audience, their topic and their approach. See the illustration below. In order to be respected and taken seriously by the audience, the speaker or messenger must meet certain character criteria. The speaker should be knowledgeable, trustworthy and clear in intention. We tend not to listen to those who speak one way and act in another way. We should be able to defend our faith easily because we are living it out. Also, people listen to those who speak effectively. Speaking from the heart and knowing God's Word intimately will give us authority and grace to share with others in an effective manner.

Messenger	• Knowledgeable • Character (trustworthy) • Intention (persuade, entertain, inform)(deceive)
Message	• Truthful • Logical • Valuable
Medium	• Oral, written, visual, by example • Involves Senses • Evokes emotions

The content of what we say is obviously important. The message should be truthful, logical and provide value to the audience. If others sense that there is no meaning or purpose to the message, it will not be well-received. Here again, knowing God's Word and letting the Holy Spirit guide the message will allow us to have a clear and powerful message. In apologetics, it is important to be familiar with sources and evidence outside of scripture that will substantiate what is in scripture, since non-believers do not accept God's Word as their foundation.

Finally, we must consider the manner in which we are presenting our case or message. Most often this will involve communication through speaking to others. Often a good conversation can be followed up with references to scriptures for people to consider mediating on. We can also share other resources that might help them obtain more answers. Be prepared for someone to ask you tell them more or to point them to the next steps.

As a parallel, we can note that Jesus is all 3 in 1. He was the Messenger, the Message and the Medium who delivered it.

Messenger (The Word)	• The word made flesh • I am the way and the truth and the life • God's Promise for Salvation
Message (The Word)	• In the beginning was the word- spoke everything into existence • We cannot live on bread alone but on every word that proceeds from the Father • Jesus did not speak anything that the Father did not tell him
Medium (The Word)	• Sword of the spirit, fought Satan with "it is written" • Living word- role model, sacrifice • Scripture and Holy Spirit

As we proceed, I offer this disclaimer. A single chapter dedicated to this topic cannot do it justice, I sincerely encourage you to do additional research on the principles addressed in this chapter. Study and show yourself approved (2 Timothy 2:15). There are countless books and courses about the topic of apologetics, so where should we begin? At the beginning! The first case we could argue for is the existence of God Himself. You cannot share the salvation of Christ with someone who doubts God's existence. For this we need to consider The Book of Genesis. What evidence do we have for God's existence?

The beginning of scripture sets up that God created the universe and everything in it. We are all here reading this now, so we know that the universe exists. Physics can explain that the universe in fact exists. What it cannot do is provide direct evidence for the who or how it was created. Scriptures fill in these missing pieces. God says He created it and He says that it was spoken into being.

It is not logical or scientific to assume that things merely exist out of nothing. There is always a cause. Keep in mind, causes are not always seen, but we can elude to them in the fact that we can observe the results. It is highly unplausible that our grand universe and all of its creation sprung into existence uncaused. Therefore, its beginning is causal. If it is causal, then there must be a cause. The cause is creation. It was created by something supernatural outside of the universe itself, which tells us there is a creator. This is a synopsis of the Kalam Cosmological Argument. It uses logic and scientific reasoning to extrapolate that the evidence leads to an intentional cause for the beginning of the universe. The Creator wanted to create it, so He did with the intention to connect with His creation.

Our Creator, God is a god of order. His order is evident in everything in creation. Psalm 19:1 tells us, "The heavens declare the glory of God; the skies proclaim the work of his hands". Down to the human genome, we can see an intricate order and attention to detail that cannot be left to chance. There is evidence to support intelligent design. This is even difficult for atheists to refute. Everything has an intention and purpose in such a definitive way. This points to the fact that everything was created by a personal creator who had a purpose.

Furthermore, we are born with an innate sense to connect nature to a creator. All of creation shows us who He is. Those who deny this fact are rejecting God at the most fundamental level.

Jon Amos Comenius, a well-known pastor in the 1600s, who is also influential in the area of education, once said, "nature is God's second book." When taking in all of scripture, all of the evidence from nature and considering logical reasoning, it all points to the fact that the universe was created and that God is the creator.

The next defense is about the authority of The Word. This is essential if we are to use scripture to back up anything that we say. As a believer we take it on faith that The Bible is the divinely inspired Word of God. For those without faith, it is just another story written by humans. However, 99% of what is in The Bible can be corroborated by other outside sources. This lends validity to scripture when used as a historical reference point. Through textual criticism, we have substantial evidence to validate the date and accuracy of the books of The Bible. There is both internal and external evidence that supports the accuracy of scripture.

As for evidence that it is inspired by God, that comes from the fact that the Word can be tested and come back as truth every time. The Word is also timeless and unchanging. It is the most published, translated and read text of all human history. These things cannot be said about any other text, past or present. No other text intricately intertwines every aspect of daily life and offers a rational and practical justification for the human condition.

How do we know the truth about Jesus? What evidence is there about Him? And was He who He said He was? There is no debate that there is overwhelming evidence that historically Jesus lived. There is also no doubt that historically Jesus died. There is historical reliability for the gospels and countless testimonies that speak to the fact of Jesus' life and death. Although there are four gospels recounting the story of Jesus' life, they are not contrary to one another; they actually complement each other. In addition, there are approximately 130 Christian and non-Christian sources outside of scripture that mention Jesus. These texts are early and have been widely accepted by critics as authentic and reliable. Based on scriptural and historical evidence, there is more evidence for Jesus' existence than against it.

Now knowing that He did in fact live and die, what proves that He also was who He claimed to be? There is also substantial evidence proving this and it is linked to His resurrection. First, there were several eyewitnesses to the events and they spoke about it immediately to others. Of the eyewitness accounts, they represent a multitude of different people, not just Jesus' followers. So, there would be no motivation at such an early date to lie or fabricate this story.

Additionally, the accounts of having seen Jesus after His death are reported early. There was not enough time to make things up and pass them along as legend.

We also have Jesus' word that He said, He is the 'Son of Man' and the 'Son of God'. These are direct quotes corroborated by scripture.

Lastly, people who had seen Him after His death were transformed. Such is the case of Saul, who then became known as Paul. The early believers became martyrs and were willing to die for their belief. People are not willing to die for something they believe to be a lie.

Some of the most compelling of all evidence for the resurrection lies in that fact that all other theories fail to yield justification for the facts that we do have as mentioned above. To date, there have been a dozen other supposed theories about what could have happened to Jesus' body. Some could be plausible while others are just ridiculous. Upon further examination of these theories, they can all be refuted based on the solid facts that we do have. Therefore, all the facts naturally fit with the best theory, that in fact, Jesus did rise from the dead. And because we can say this, we then know that everything else He said was also true.

In John 8:49-50, Jesus is explaining to the Pharisees who He was, and He says, "I Am". This relates back to Exodus 3:14 when Moses is speaking to God and asks Him, who should I say has sent me. God responded, "I Am". Therefore, Jesus himself tells us He is God.

Having some evidence about the three most disputed claims of Christianity sets us up to contend for the faith. So how do present this to others?

First and foremost, if someone makes a claim, they need to justify it. It is not for us to provide proof of their belief, it is for them to support it, or to disprove our belief. There is no doubt that we will be met with opposition when engaging in this type of discourse. There are several tested tactics that will support our efforts to defend the faith in these moments.

The person who makes the claim has to defend it, so we can dismantle claims against Christianity by asking good questions that will lead the other person to challenge their own ideas and beliefs. If you put the burden of proof on them to explain their position, you will find they slowly loosen their grip on what they think they know. This does not need to be aggressive in nature. The questions can be general interest and probing questions to bring light to the other person's perspective. Often others have not really considered why they believe what they do, let alone have evidence to back it up. Christianity has a ton of evidence to support it. Ask others for their evidence.

The second tactic is known as the 'suicide' tactic. If someone poses an incorrect claim, let them use their own criteria and thinking that they set forth to address the arguments. The further they go with their erroneous thinking, it will become evident that their claim is self-refuting. Another similar tactic is called 'taking the roof off'. This is when we can push a person's claim to its obvious conclusion therefore exposing the fact that they cannot actually live out the claim that they are making.

Both of these tactics are good for refuting moral issues and claims related to relativism.

We can also appeal to the 'just the facts' tactic. This is to remove emotions, religion, and personal attachments to the claims and just objectively review the evidence and facts. This is tricky sometimes because people cannot fully disconnect from their personal viewpoints and deeply held convictions. However, fact after fact can be held up against each other based on their own merits. If sincerely using logical reasoning, the truth will win out.

So, let us be steadfast in sharing our faith with confidence as Jude 3 (NKJV) tells us, "Beloved, while I was very diligent to write to you concerning our common salvation, I found it necessary to write to you exhorting you to contend earnestly for the faith which was once for all delivered to the saints". Make a commitment and be prepared to share and defend the faith on every occasion.

This chapter was a toe in the water of apologetics. There are great resources at the end of this chapter that will help you explore it more fully. With all this said, let's keep in mind that people don't generally come to the faith because it is rational or because they had one 'divine experience'. People generally come to the faith because they are among witnesses who are living the faith. If we live a life that honors God and puts Jesus as the center, we will have a life that others will want too.

Then they will be prompted to ask us about our beliefs. It is for that moment when we should be prepared to share. Let people see Jesus in us and the hope we have in Him. This is the ultimate defense for our faith.

For Your Heart

- *Be prepared to give an explanation of your faith at any time.*
- *Seek opportunities to lead others in truth and correct misguided thinking.*
- *Be prepared for opposition and resistance.*

For Your Spirit

Thank you, God that you have given me cause for hope in Jesus Christ, and because of this good news, I can joyfully proclaim it before others. I know that when I am faced with a giant, your Word and Spirit will guide me and protect me. May I never have a spirit of fear or shame in proclaiming your mighty name, but speak boldly before others. In Jesus' name I pray. -Amen

For Your Mind

Confound The Critics- Answers for Attacks on Biblical Truths, Bodie Hodge (2014) Master Books. AR.

Evidence That Demands a Verdict: Life Changing Truth for a Skeptical World, Josh McDowell (2017) Thomas Nelson Publishing. TN

The Lie, Ken Ham (1987) Master Books. AR

Foxe's Book of Martyrs, John Foxe (updated 2016) Bridge-Logos. FL.

Mere Christianity, C.S. Lewis (1943) MacMillan Publishing Company. NY.

Meeting Jesus Again for the First Time, Marcus J. Borg (1995) Harper Collins. NY.

Stand to Reason Organization by Greg Koukl-
https://www.str.org/

Conclusion

"And now, Lord, look upon their threats and grant to your servants to continue to speak your word with all boldness,"

Acts 4:29 (ESV)

Knowing God, embracing His Holy Spirit and acknowledging who He has made us to be is how we become powerful and effective. Walking in truth and speaking love needs to be our game plan. This will require us to re-commit and submit to Him each day. This is not something we can do alone. Satan is the king of distraction. He is looking for any place he can take us off course. We must not lose focus or strength in this hour. Daily renewing of our mind and spirit will give us strength and guidance for each trial that is before us. A reminder that I have been using to stay on course is 3T model illustrated below.

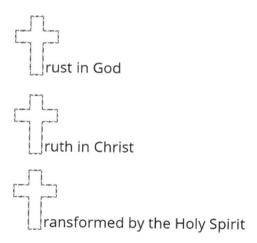

rust in God

ruth in Christ

ransformed by the Holy Spirit

This helps us to align our priorities and get back to our purpose. We cannot control the circumstances around us, but if we believe as we say, then we know who is in control. Being able to rest in God's sovereignty, our redemption in Christ and the guidance from the Holy Spirit gives us the ability to not only survive, but thrive as a Christian in a post-Christian culture.

One thing is for sure: we cannot be driven by fear. Although society is pushing fear in every form, we know that we were not given a spirit of fear. Regardless of our viewpoints on any worldly matter, the real issue is misplaced fear. There is nothing this world can threaten us with that the cross has not already won victory over. Our only fear should be of God, and a fear of life without Him. Everything is in His control and will fall into place according to His Will.

We were saved by Christ, not to be safe, but to reach out and impact others. We cannot hide ourselves away and insulate ourselves from the ills of this world. We must be the salt and light wherever it is that God has placed us. We are more effective in doing this when we gather as a body of believers and unite together in mind, body and spirit. Now is the time that we should seek out those who are like-minded and truly commit to encouraging one another in the journey.

Recall the story of Moses and the Amalekites from Exodus 17. Moses calls for Aaron and Hur to join him on the top of the hill to watch the battle being fought below.

Whenever Moses had his hands raised, the Israelites were winning. As soon as Moses lowered his hands, the Amalekites gained ground. So, Moses with all his might stood at the top of the hill holding his hands up in support of the Israelites. When Moses' strength was giving out, Aaron and Hur came alongside him and propped Moses up on each side. They helped Moses hold his arms up until sunset, and the Amalekites were defeated. Imagine if we were in a battle so important, so draining that we physically could not stand, yet we knew there would be someone to stand beside us literally propping us up so we could not fail. With God before us and people like that beside us, there is nothing we cannot overcome.

We are not fully ready for battle without putting on the armor of God daily. This helps us become mentally and spiritually prepared in our walk to endure and overcome the challenges in life. God equipped us to be victorious both in the natural and into eternity. Central to this process is regular communication with the Commander-In-Chief through prayer. Tuning into what God says both through His Word and through His Spirit gives us strategy for our victory.

Furthermore, after experiencing big and small victories each day, we should be able to stand firm to defend the faith in which we have built. Being able to know what we believe, why we believe it and effectively communicate that to others helps us impact their walk with Christ. This not only strengthens us but is effective for advancing the Kingdom of God.

We do not have to have all the answers or be the most confident, or even have the most faith. We just need a willingness to allow God to work through us. This requires less of self and more of Him. Sometimes we can be most effective by simply getting out of our own way so God can do His thing. The process of becoming powerful and effective for God's Kingdom starts with one step. Each time we are faithful in a small step, God will introduce us to a bigger step, paving the way for ultimate transformation in our own life and larger impact to the people around us.

I encourage you to make that first step. God has given you all the abilities and tools required for this journey. You need only say, 'Yes'. I pray that God meets you where you are and gives you the confidence you need to proclaim His Word with boldness to everyone who needs to hear it. I hope this book has been a blessing to you and gives you encouragement to live powerfully for God.

I'll close with the words of 2 Timothy 3 (ESV):

But understand this, that in the last days there will come times of difficulty. [2] For people will be lovers of self, lovers of money, proud, arrogant, abusive, disobedient to their parents, ungrateful, unholy, [3] heartless, unappeasable, slanderous, without self-control, brutal, not loving good, [4] treacherous, reckless, swollen with conceit, lovers of pleasure rather than lovers of God, [5] having the appearance of godliness, but denying its power. Avoid such people.

⁶ For among them are those who creep into households and capture weak women, burdened with sins and led astray by various passions, ⁷ always learning and never able to arrive at a knowledge of the truth. ⁸ Just as Jannes and Jambres opposed Moses, so these men also oppose the truth, men corrupted in mind and disqualified regarding the faith. ⁹ But they will not get very far, for their folly will be plain to all, as was that of those two men.

¹⁰ You, however, have followed my teaching, my conduct, my aim in life, my faith, my patience, my love, my steadfastness, ¹¹ my persecutions and sufferings that happened to me at Antioch, at Iconium, and at Lystra— which persecutions I endured; yet from them all the Lord rescued me. ¹² Indeed, all who desire to live a godly life in Christ Jesus will be persecuted, ¹³ while evil people and impostors will go on from bad to worse, deceiving and being deceived. ¹⁴ But as for you, continue in what you have learned and have firmly believed, knowing from whom you learned it ¹⁵ and how from childhood you have been acquainted with the sacred writings, which are able to make you wise for salvation through faith in Christ Jesus. ¹⁶ All Scripture is breathed out by God and profitable for teaching, for reproof, for correction, and for training in righteousness, ¹⁷ that the man of God may be complete, equipped for every good work.

If you have never accepted Jesus to truly be the way, the truth and the life in your journey, I encourage you to make that decision now. All you need to do is invite Him in. There is no script to repeat and no contract to sign.

All that is needed is a pure heart that desires Him to rescue you. Approach Him like a friend, admit that you have fallen into sin and want to repent from your old ways. Embrace the love, forgiveness, redemption and freedom that Jesus is extending to you now.

Jesus please be near to those who want to receive you now. Touch the hearts and minds of those in need of you. Thank you for the transformation that you will begin in them. I pray the power of the Holy Spirit will move them in a mighty way. It is in your precious name that I agree in prayer for this person. – Amen

Appendices

Included here are additional resources to encourage and equip you.

Further Meditations

Do I speak truth in love? Truth is essential but only when spoken in love.

Do I worship in spirit and truth? Worship is powerful when done in spirit and truth

Do I know what I stand for? We stand firm when we know what we stand for!

Do I live like I am a follower of Christ? It's not enough to just know the Word of God, we must believe it is truth and do what it says!

Satan is working overtime, am I? Don't give up any ground!

God is for you, are you for Him? He must be the center of our lives.

What are you a vessel of? We are a vessel so we will ultimately be filled with something, if it is not God's word and His spirit, it will be something of the world.

Quick Steps to Leading Others to Christ

Care
- Smile- be calm and gentle
- Show geniune concern-its not about winning an arguement its about winning a soul!

Connect
- Share a testimony
- Ask them what they believe-listen attentively
- Ask them, if what they believe in was incorrect would they want to know the truth?

Contend
- Share Romans 3:23, 6:23- we have all sinned an fallen short, sin is death
- Share Romans 5:8, Romans 10:9-10 - The redemptive work through Jesus

Close
- If there is opportunity- ask them when they die, do they know where they are going? Share that belief in Jesus guarantees we will be with God in heaven
- Pray with them- if they refuse, pray for them.

Daily Encouragement For Developing Discernment

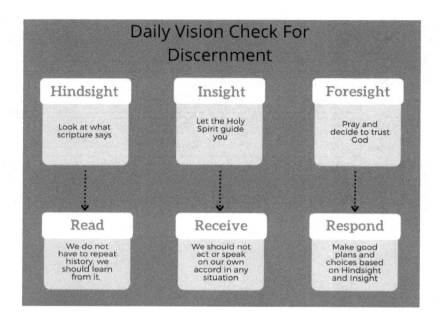

Bible References (in order of presentation)

Psalm 22:22	John 8:47	James 3:17
1 Corinthians 9:16 ESV	John 10:27-28	John 17:16
John 15:19	James 1:22	James 4:4
Matthew 7:13-14	John 1:12-13	Romans 12:2
Acts 2:21	Ephesians 6:7	1 Corinthians 1:10
Matthew 5:15	2 Timothy 1:7	Romans 15:5
John 17:15	John 8:31-32	Jude 4
Exodus 3:14	John 16:33	1 John 4:1
Isaiah 55:8-9	Mark 12:30	Matthew 7:21-23
1 John 4:19	2 Corinthians 5:20	James 3:1
John 21:16	Philippians 1:27-28	Proverbs 4:25-27
Colossians 3:23	Matthew 22:29	Joshua 1:7-10
Romans 8:28	Philippians 4:8	Psalm 118:8
Psalm 139:7-10	Matthew 6:24	Romans 8:31
Psalm 147:5	Titus 3:14	Proverbs 4:23
Jeremiah 32:27	James 1:27	1 Peter 2:9
Colossians 1:16-17	Philippians 2:3-4	Revelations 2:1-3:22

Acts 17:24-31	Matthew 14	John 6:63
Isaiah 55:6-7	Acts 16	1 Corinthians 6:19
James 1:17	John 17:14-20	Genesis 1
Hebrews 12:28	Proverbs 4:25-27	Ephesians 6:12
Luke 10:27	Matthew 6:33	John 14:26
	John 10:17-18	

John 15:26	Proverbs 4	Psalm 46:1
Acts 1:8	James 1	Isaiah 55:11
1 Corinthians	Hosea 4:6	Hebrews 4:12
4:19-20	1 Corinthians	Luke 22:31-32
2 Corinthians 3:17	3:18-19	James 5:16
Job 33:4	Proverbs 18:20-21	Matthew 6:9-13
Psalm 119:11	Ephesians 4:15	1 Thessalonians
Luke 12:10-12	Ephesians 4:29	5:16-18
1 Corinthians 12:7	Colossians 4:6	Philippians 4:6
1 Peter 4:10	Matthew 12:37	Hebrews 4:16
Isaiah 11:2-3	1 Peter 3:10	1 John 5:15

Romans 12:6	Proverbs 15:4	Matthew 21:22
1 Corinthians 12	Luke 12:8-9	Isaiah 54:17
Galatians 5:22-23	Matthew 11:28-30	1 Peter 3:15
Ephesians 4:11	Romans 10:17	2 Timothy 4:2-5
Matthew 12:36	John 3:16	Colossians 4:5
Matthew 15:18	Acts 4:13	Matthew 16:13
Proverbs 16:24	Mark 16:15	Proverbs 15:1
James 3:5	Acts 28:31	2 Timothy 2:15
Genesis 11:5-7	Ephesians 6:10-11	John 8:49-50
Job 1:20	John 10:10	Jude 3
2 Kings 4	John 8:44	Acts 4:29
Psalm 1:1-6	1 John 3:8	Exodus 17
	Ephesians 6:14-17	2 Timothy 3

Bibliography (in order of presentation)

W.A. Pratney, *The Nature and Character of God* (Michigan: Bethany House Publishers, 1988)

John Van Diest, *10 Things Satan Doesn't Want you to Know* (Colorado: Multnomah Publishers, 1998)

John Ellis, *The Breakdown of Higher Education* (NY: Encounter Books, 2021)

Andy Andrews, *How Do You Kill 11 Million People? Why The Truth Matters More Than You Think* (TN: Thomas Nelson Publishing, 2011)

David Horowitz, *The Dark Agenda- The War to Destroy Christian America* (FL: Humanix Books, 2018)

Mike Gonzalez, *The Plot to Change America- How Identity Politics is Dividing the Land of the Free* (NY: Encounter Books, 2020)

Leo Tolstoy, *The Law of Love and The Law of Violence* (NY: Rudolph Field, 1948)

O.S. Hawkins, *The Jesus Code* (TN: Thomas Nelson Publishing, 2016)

Alisa Childers, *Another Gospel ?-* (IL: Tyndale, 2020)

J.C. Ryle, *Holiness: Its Nature, Hindrances, Difficulties and Roots* (MA: Hendrickson Publishers, 2007)

A.W. Tozer, *How to be filled with the Holy Spirit* (NY: Moody's, 2016)

Eugene H. Peterson, *Tell It Slant- a conversation on the language of Jesus in his stories and prayers* (MI: Eerdmans Publishing, 2008)

Diane Ravitch, *The Language Police-How Pressure Groups Restrict What Students Learn* (NY: Vintage Books, 2003)

Nabeel Qureshi, *Seeking Allah Finding Jesus: A Devout Muslim Encounters Christianity* (MI: Zondervan Books, 2014)

Rifqa Bary, *Hiding in the Light* (CO: Waterbrook Press, 2015)

Mark Stuart, *Losing My Voice to Find It: How A Rock Star Discovered His Greatest Purpose,* (TN: Thomas Nelson Publishing, 2019)

Elizabeth Alves, *Becoming A Prayer Warrior- A Guide to Effective and Powerful Prayer* (CA: Regal Books, 1998)

Bodie Hodge, *Confound The Critics- Answers for Attacks on Biblical Truths* (AR: Master Books, 2014)

Josh McDowell, *Evidence That Demands a Verdict: Life Changing Truth for a Skeptical World* (TN: Thomas Nelson Publishing, 2017)

Ken Ham, *The Lie* (AR: Master Books, 1987)

John Foxe, *Foxe's Book of Martyrs* (FL: Bridge-Logos, updated 2016)

C.S. Lewis, *Mere Christianity* (NY: MacMillan Publishing Company, 1943)

Marcus J. Borg, *Meeting Jesus Again for the First Time* (NY: Harper Collins, 1995)

Other Resources

https://www.barna.com/research/changing-state-of-the-church/

Stand to Reason, https://www.str.org/

2009 Tim Tebow Quote, https://fanbuzz.com/college-football/sec/florida/tim-tebow-john-316/

One Nail, https://bible.org/illustration/one-nail

CPSIA information can be obtained
at www.ICGtesting.com
Printed in the USA
JSHW040941310722
28678JS00006B/115

9 781957 294056